Edward John Hardy

Faint, Yet Pursuing

And Other Sermons

Edward John Hardy

Faint, Yet Pursuing
And Other Sermons

ISBN/EAN: 9783337160555

Printed in Europe, USA, Canada, Australia, Japan

Cover: Foto ©Lupo / pixelio.de

More available books at **www.hansebooks.com**

FAINT, YET PURSUING

BY THE SAME AUTHOR.

Presentation Editions, 7s. 6d.; Popular Editions, 3s. 6d. each.

HOW TO BE HAPPY THOUGH MARRIED.

BEING A HANDBOOK TO MARRIAGE.

Sixth Edition.

"We strongly recommend this book as one of the best of wedding presents. It is a complete handbook to an earthly Paradise, and its author may be regarded as the Murray of Matrimony and the Baedeker of Bliss."—*Pall Mall Gazette*.

"The author has successfully accomplished a difficult task in writing a clever and practical book on the important subject of matrimony. . . . This book, which is at once entertaining and full of wise precepts, deserves to be widely read."—*Morning Post*.

"MANNERS MAKYTH MAN."

Second Edition.

"Good-natured, wholesome, and straightforward."—*Saturday Review*.

"A really delightful volume, well adapted for family reading."—*Christian World*.

LONDON:
T. FISHER UNWIN, 26, PATERNOSTER SQUARE, E.C.

FAINT, YET PURSUING

AND OTHER SERMONS

BY

EDWARD J. HARDY, M.A

Chaplain to H.M. Forces

"Man! what is this, and why art thou despairing?
God will forgive thee all but thy despair"

London
T. FISHER UNWIN
26 PATERNOSTER SQUARE
MDCCCLXXXVIII

To

THE CONGREGATION (CHURCH OF ENGLAND)

WORSHIPPING IN

THE CHAPEL OF THE ROYAL VICTORIA HOSPITAL, NETLEY,

THESE SERMONS ARE DEDICATED WITH

THE BEST WISHES OF THEIR

CHAPLAIN.

PREFACE.

THE publisher of "How to be Happy though Married" suggested to me that some of the many readers of that book might like to have the thoughts of the writer on more serious subjects—if there is any subject more serious than matrimony. Hence this little volume. The sermons in it have at least one merit—they are short. It is true that even a short sermon may be tiresome. We have all heard of the answer that some one gave to a clergyman who said that he had made his sermon short, and hoped that he was not tedious: "And yet you were tedious." But no clergyman can avoid being tedious to those who are bored even with the text, which is sure to be the best part of his sermon, and before anything else has followed. We must, it would seem, admit the fact that some persons are physically and morally incapable of reading or listening to sermons. It is well for them that a book of printed sermons can be so easily left unopened or shut up.

About half of these sermons were preached to soldiers, who are by no means as uninterested in religious matters as civilians sometimes give them credit for being.

Much of our apologetic theological literature may be described as the doubtful solution of doubtful doubts, and probably the last four sermons may come under this description. In them I have at least made an honest attempt to meet difficulties felt by myself.

CONTENTS.

INTRODUCTORY.

HOMILETICAL THOUGHTS.

I.

FAINT, YET PURSUING.

	PAGE
JUDGES VIII. 4.—" Faint, yet pursuing " … … … …	31

II.

THORNS IN THE FLESH.

2 CORINTHIANS XII. 7.—" And lest I should be exalted above measure through the abundance of the revelations, there was given to me a thorn in the flesh, the messenger of Satan to buffet me, lest I should be exalted above measure" … … … … … … 39

III.

THE PERFECT WORK OF PATIENCE.

JAMES I. 4.—" Let patience have her perfect work, that ye may be perfect and entire, wanting nothing" ... 47

IV.

A REFUGE FOR THE DISTRESSED.

1 SAMUEL XXII. 2.—" And every one that was in distress, and every one that was in debt, and every one that was discontented, gathered themselves unto him; and he became captain over them" 54

V.

MISTAKES ABOUT HAPPINESS.

JOHN IV. 13.—" Whosoever drinketh of this water shall thirst again: but whosoever drinketh of the water that I shall give him shall never thirst; but the water that I shall give him shall be in him a well of water springing up into everlasting life" 62

VI.

A WISE CHOICE.

1 KINGS III. 10.—" And the speech pleased the Lord, that Solomon had asked this thing" 69

VII.

THE DAY OF SALVATION.

LUKE XVIII. 37.—" And they told him that Jesus of Nazareth passeth by" 77

VIII.

SISERA NO MATCH FOR THE STARS.

JUDGES V. 20.—" They fought from heaven ; the stars in their courses fought against Sisera " 85

IX.

THE BABYLONIAN CAPTIVITY.

PSALM CXXXVII. 3.—" They that carried us away captive required of us a song " 95

X.

EJACULATORY PRAYER.

NEHEMIAH II. 4.—" So I prayed to the God of heaven " 106

XI.

GOD'S METHOD OF PUNISHMENT.

PROVERBS I. 31.—" Therefore shall they eat of the fruit of their own way, and be filled with their own devices " 114

XII.

OUR FATHER'S CHASTISEMENT.

PSALM LI. 7.—" Purge me with hyssop, and I shall be clean "... 123

XIII.

CHRISTIAN FRIENDSHIP.

MALACHI III. 16.—"Then they that feared the Lord spake often one to another: and the Lord hearkened and heard it, and a book of remembrance was written before Him for them that feared the Lord, and that thought upon His name" 130

XIV.

THOUGHTS FOR ADVENT.

JOB XVI. 22.—"When a few years are come, then I shall go the way whence I shall not return" 138

XV.

MORE THOUGHTS FOR ADVENT.

JEREMIAH XXXVI. 22, 23.—"Now the king sat in the winter-house in the ninth month: and there was a fire on the hearth burning before him. And it came to pass, that when Jehudi had read three or four leaves, he cut it with the penknife, and cast it into the fire that was on the hearth, until all the roll was consumed in the fire that was on the hearth" 144

XVI.

CHRISTMAS THOUGHTS.

LUKE II. 7.—"There was no room in the inn" 151

XVII.

THE DIVINE ARITHMETIC OF LIFE.

PSALM XC. 12.—"So teach us to number our days, that we may apply our hearts unto wisdom" 159

XVIII.

EXCUSES.

GENESIS III. 12, 13.—"And the man said, The woman whom Thou gavest to be with me, she gave me of the tree, and I did eat. And the Lord God said unto the woman, What is this that thou hast done? And the woman said, The serpent beguiled me, and I did eat" 167

XIX.

SECRET FAULTS.

PSALM XIX. 12.—"Who can understand his errors? cleanse thou me from secret faults" 173

XX.

"IS IT NOT A LITTLE ONE?"

GENESIS XIX. 20.—"I cannot escape to the mountain, lest evil overtake me, and I die: behold now, this city is near to flee unto, and it is a little one: Oh, let me escape thither (is it not a little one?) and my soul shall live" 180

XXI.

FOREWARNED FOREARMED.

1 CORINTHIANS X. 11.—"Wherefore let him that thinketh he standeth take heed lest he fall' 190

XXII.
NO WASTE.

JOHN VI. 12.—"Gather up the fragments that remain, that nothing be lost" ... 198

XXIII.
GOOD FRIDAY AND BAD FRIDAY.

LUKE XXIV.—"Thus it is written, and thus it behoved Christ to suffer, and to rise from the dead the third day: And that repentance and remission of sins should be preached in His name among all nations, beginning at Jerusalem" ... 208

XXIV.
THE FULL, PERFECT, AND SUFFICIENT SACRIFICE.

JOHN XII. 24.—"Verily, verily, I say unto you, Except a corn of wheat fall into the ground and die, it abideth alone: but if it die it bringeth forth much fruit" ... 215

XXV.
VOLUNTEER FOR GOD.

JOHN VII. 17.—"If any man will do His will, he shall know of the doctrine, whether it be of God" ... 224

XXVI.
THE LORD AND GIVER OF LIFE.

1 JOHN V. 12.—"He that hath the Son hath life; and he that hath not the Son of God hath not life" ... 231

XXVII.

WORLDLINESS.

1 JOHN II. 15.—" If any man love the world, the love of the Father is not in him " 236

XXVIII.

BID CHRIST TO YOUR WEDDING.

JOHN II. 2.—"And both Jesus was called, and His disciples, to the marriage" 245

XXIX.

OLD TESTAMENT HEROES.

HEBREWS XI. 32-38.—"Gideon, Barak, Samson, Jephthah, David, Samuel, and the prophets . . . . of whom the world was not worthy" 250

XXX.

ARE CHRISTIAN PRINCIPLES PRACTICAL?

MATTHEW V. 39, 42; VI. 25.—"But I say unto you, that ye resist not evil; but whosoever shall smite thee on the right cheek, turn to him the other also. Give to him that asketh thee, and from him that would borrow of thee turn not thou away. Therefore I say unto you, Take no thought (Be not anxious, R.V.) for your life, what ye shall eat, or what ye shall drink; nor yet for your body, what ye shall put on". 258

XXXI.

CHRISTIAN SOCIALISM.

LUKE XII. 13, 14, 15.—"And one of the company said unto Him, Master, speak to my brother, that he divide the inheritance with me. And He said unto him, Man, who made Me a judge or a divider over you? And He said unto them, Take heed and beware of covetousness" 266

XXXII.

SEEING NOT NECESSARILY BELIEVING.

JOHN VI. 36.—"But I said unto you, that ye also have seen me, and believe not" 276

INTRODUCTION.

HOMILETICAL THOUGHTS.[1]

WHEN one sees in the newspapers accounts of the Salvation Army having " knee drill " at different places, which is followed by addresses, at each of which ten or a dozen of the greatest sinners are converted, and several hundreds nearly so; or when a friendly Dissenter tells you that every sermon should be followed by a striking effect, and that you are to be pitied if you do not see results and have not very frequently the luxury of leading souls to

---

[1] This essay formed the substance of a paper read to a Clerical Society and printed in *The Clergyman's Magazine.* It is now reprinted as an introduction to a volume of sermons to illustrate the difficulty of turning theory into practice. The sermons are the practice, the essay is the theory, and how far he is from practising what he preaches in the matter of composing sermons as in every other respect no one knows better than the writer of these " Homiletical Thoughts."

Christ; or when in the "silly season," for want of better news, the newspapers inform the British public that preaching in the Church of England has become a lost art, and that we of the clergy are, as regards this sort of influence, and as compared with writers for the press, mere frauds (to speak with brutal plainness), what, I ask, is Othello to say or do when not only those who sit in the seat of the scornful, but candid friends assure him that his occupation is gone? Is he to bear with indifference such taunts as that of the barrister (which is but the echo of what many other educated *men* are saying), "A whole week to get up the case, and no reply from the other side, and—I don't think much of it"? But, Mr. Barrister, few clergymen *have* "a whole week to get up the case," for there is no class of men more pressed for time than the majority of the clergy. This is one reason why sermons are not more effective. We have heard it said that an unprepared sermon is like schism, either a necessity or a sin; but to how many hard-working clergy is it not the former!

Though some barristers are not very complimentary in their remarks about sermons, may we not get hints from the style of speaking adopted by the bar? One barrister was asked why he kept hammering away so long at one point. He replied, "Because I could not get that stupid fellow in the corner of the jury-box to see it sooner." Ought not preachers to do their work in the same practical way? Again, barristers do what preachers often fail to do—they *make points*. When they have got hold of a good point they do not leave it until every juryman not only hears it, but sees it. And even when they have a bad case (which preachers need never have) how much some barristers contrive to make out of it! A great French lawyer was employed to defend a murderer against whom the facts were hopelessly clear. When his pathetic appeals and his tears failed to touch his stolid audience, he resorted to the most impudent piece of broad farce. He made all sorts of jokes and bombastic appeals. The jury responded with loud and uncontrolled bursts of laughter. This was the advocate's opportunity. Feigning high moral indignation at their conduct, he continued, "You are about to decide whether one of your fellow-men shall be thrust by you out of the ranks of the living, and you choose such a moment for indulging in cruel and thoughtless laughter. Is this extravagant mirth a fitting mood in which to decide whether a man shall or shall not die?" The argument actually told on the jury. The man was acquitted. Certainly preachers should be far more particular than this lawyer was in the use of means, but ought they not to strive as earnestly for practical results?

Nor ought we to be afraid of using anecdotes and similes that may cause a smile. Do not smiles come from God as much as tears? He was a wise Welsh preacher who used to make his congregation laugh on purpose, for, said he, "I can more easily make the bucket tilt over on the other side." Most of us must have observed that stupid, uneducated people smile with pleasure and surprise when the meaning of a speaker's words dawns upon them. George Eliot says very truly that such take anything they understand for wit. A smile, then, is often nothing more than the receipt which is given to a preacher for remarks received with understanding—a grateful acknowledgment for some happy hit, or for great plainness of speech, which is the foundation of real eloquence, but which makes people smile with surprise because it is so unusual. We should certainly be so dignified as never to become vulgar, but never so dignified as to make our pulpits die of dignity. Of course care must be taken not to fall into the "state of anecdotage," and to avoid anecdotes that are manifestly untrue.

The actor's reply is well known when asked why his words, which were not true, affected an audience more than the preacher's words, which are true. "Because I say what is false as if it were true, while you say what is true as if it were false." We speak with emotion when informed that our chimney is on fire, but we are quite calm, if not indifferent, when preaching about temperance, righteousness, and the judgment to come.

An old barrister was giving advice to his son, who was just entering his father's profession. "My son," said the counsellor, "if you have a case where the law is clearly on your side, but justice seems to be clearly against you, urge upon the jury the vast importance of sustaining the law. If, on the other hand, you are in doubt about the law, but your client's case is founded on justice, insist on the necessity of doing justice, though the heavens fall." " But," asked the son, " how shall I manage a case where law and justice are dead against me ? " " In that case," replied the old man, " talk round it." If from some barristers we may learn how to do it, from this one we may learn how *not* to do it. We must not talk round our subjects, nor preach before people instead of to them.

Of course we all wish our sermons to be practical. We want to hit something or somebody by aiming at something or somebody. We would not be like those who beat the air. Certainly the common people will not hear us gladly if we utter nothing but abstract platitudes—things hard to be understood, and quite unconnected with their business and bosoms. Nor will the " better classes," so called, be benefited by a preacher, however " popular," of whom it may be said, in the words of the prophet Ezekiel, " And lo, thou art unto them as a very lovely song of one that hath a pleasant voice, and can play well on an instrument: for they hear thy words, but they do them not."

There are many kinds of preaching, all of which may be practical. It will depend on the character of the preacher's own mind as well as on the congregation to which he ministers which kind is most practical. In the New Testament the preacher's office was that of a herald. He had to proclaim the good news of the kingdom and of its King. We all know the terrible difficulties that stood in the way of the first heralds of the gospel; but at least in this respect they had easier work than their successors of the nineteenth century. They had not to contend with the "disease of not marking," with which our congregations are afflicted by reason of their familiarity with the "old, old story." It was news to the crowds who heard St. Peter and St. Paul proclaiming it for the first time, and as such was eagerly listened to. *They* had congregations who were not "gospel-hardened." How are we to make up for this loss of novelty? What is the best way of putting our message to people who have heard it from infancy?

It is not enough to say that it is the same gospel now, and that, therefore, it should have the same effect, however familiar it is. In the first place, we know that the best story is spoiled if badly told, and that good style in literature is necessary for conveying good matter. I have heard the American evangelist Mr. Moody, and his manner and words were as practical when preaching as when in early days he sold boots in a store. Contrast such heralding with that of the parson who said what he ought to say over (very far over) the head of Tennyson's northern farmer.

To be a practical preacher it is necessary to acquire

the art of putting from time to time new setting round the pearl of great price. To do this we must endeavour to understand the actual thoughts and feelings of people living not in the time of the apostles, but in our own time. And these actual thoughts and feelings should be spoken of in language of week-day life. It is a great mistake to give our audiences credit for knowing more than they do know.

An Oxford professor, who was going to preach for a country clergyman, composed a sermon so plain that he thought every word must be understood. " I am sure there was no word that could give any difficulty in that sermon," he said to the country clergyman on coming with him out of church. The latter replied by saying to a passing parishioner, " John, can you tell me the meaning of the word *felicity* that occurred in the sermon?" "I don't rightly know, sir, but I think it be's some part in the inside of a pig." Besides technical terms, we must avoid stereotyped pulpit phrases that have become blunt and abstract expressions, which do not convey any distinct meaning even to ourselves.

We must not fancy that we are preaching Christ, and that therefore our sermons are practical, if we merely use the word " Christ " very often. For what is meant by preaching Christ? Surely not any one doctrine, but the whole of His revelation—His life as well as His death, the spirit of Christ quite as much as His actual words and deeds.

After proclaiming the good news of the kingdom, the next thing to be done is to exhort people to live worthy of their high calling. What, then, is the most practical way of preaching righteousness? Sydney Smith referred to a way of doing this which is *not* practical when he asked if sin was to be taken from man, as Eve was from Adam, by casting them into a deep slumber. Why is it that preachers of righteousness are so dull and useless? Because we speak of righteousness and unrighteousness too much in the abstract. Lately I read a pamphlet by a celebrated medical man in which he says that the clergy should teach the people, not in general terms, but in detail, the terrible punishments that follow physical sins even in this world. He would have preachers describe the horrors of drunkenness, the dismal days that follow late nights, the negligence and culpable ignorance that prevail in reference to health, the awful sin of adulterating food, and the mystery of iniquity that lies in building houses of which "every brick is a lie." We have alluded to this medical criticism not because we think it would be well to turn sermons into sanitary essays, but because it protests against mere abstract preaching, and because it is well to see ourselves as others see us, and to receive hints from all quarters.

That sermons on besetting sins may do good is, however, an undoubted fact. It is related of a certain sermon about cheating, that when an old woman who heard it was asked what she thought of the preacher, she replied, " I did not like him at all, for when I returned home I had to destroy my quart measure." I think, however, that indirect rather than direct inculcation of morality is best. It is so easy to place the cap that fits on the head of a neighbour, instead of on our own head. Besides, there is a certain pleasing excitement in being abused, which may render a satirical preacher more popular than useful. One of Swift's ironical arguments against abolishing Christianity was that sins would cease to charm if they were not abused and called wicked at least once a week.

The term casuistry has a bad name, but ought not cases of conscience to be sometimes studied and explained in the pulpit? Many people mean well, but do not know what is the right thing to be done in difficult circumstances. It is not enough to say, " Do good " and " Be good "; we should sometimes point out what good thing requires to be done, and in what respects we are to be good.

Praying, it has been said, is the end of preaching; but surely knowledge ought also to be an end aimed at. Light is required for healthy life as well as warmth. It is the preacher's duty to instruct as well as to exhort. As the first is far more difficult than the second, it is too often omitted. Craving after the signs of sensational conversions, preachers omit the less showy, but far more practical, part of their work, which consists in building up believers. Accordingly the people perish for lack of knowledge. But while avoiding the extreme of being too emotional, let us beware of the opposite fault. It is well to be logical and instructive, but these excellencies, if not counterbalanced, may make a preacher as dry as the man of whom it was said that if a hole were bored in him, nothing would come out but sawdust.

There are a few obvious but frequently forgotten rules which are *sine qua nons* of practical preaching. First we should stop when we are done. How many preachers spoil all by going on after they have proved their point. They say one more word. Just one other remark strikes them, and these "more last words" weary their audience into a bad temper, which takes the word out of their hearts. Why should a preacher turn round like a dog three times before lying down?

Another obvious rule is that we should never preach without having something to say. I once asked an old woman, whom I met returning from a Roman Catholic chapel in Ireland, whether she had heard a good sermon. "There was none," she replied. "Why?" I asked. "Oh, I suppose his riverence had nothing particular to say to us this morning." In this case it was surely wiser not to preach at all than to risk falling into the predicament of a certain Scotch minister. A matter-of-fact man, who saw him shed tears when preaching, nudged his neighbour and whispered, "What gars the minister greet?" "Hoot, man, if you were up there and had as little to say, you would cry yourself."

It seems a pity that sermons should be invariably expected even when there has not been time for adequate preparation. Certainly there is much truth in the saying that "he who preaches twice on the same day prates once." How much better it would be in such cases to borrow a good sermon, and tell the people all about it. When a sermon is very long and very dull, it is generally because enough time has not been given to its preparation. The preacher had not time to be short, that is to say to concentrate his matter, or if the sermon were extempore, perhaps no landing-place had been arranged, and the only wonder is that land should ever be reached. As a rule, people attend very well when they get something to attend to.

If we would be really practical preachers, we must not "preach cream and live skim-milk." At the same time, mere goodness will never become a substitute for brains and honest preparation. When St. Paul speaks of the foolishness of preaching, we know that he does not mean foolish preaching. If God can make preaching useful without our knowledge, He can do so even more without our ignorance. Some say that all that is required is to throw ourselves upon God, and that He will make our sermons useful; but we know that God only helps those who help themselves.

In conclusion, let me suggest a few queries for the consideration of my readers. The first is, Has preaching in the Church of England failed owing to the spread of education and other causes, as Professor Mahaffy seems to think in a book he published called " Decay of Modern Preaching " ? Certainly people do not now listen to sermons as eagerly as they did when, long ago, a whole congregation stood up and asked the preacher on more than one occasion to turn his hour-glass and preach a second hour. A long sermon is now considered little less than a social impropriety.

Is there not too much sameness about our preaching, and does not the conventionality of the pulpit prevent many sermons from being more practical? How is it that the same sermon may be preached by different men with almost opposite effects? Are some preachers more highly charged magnetic batteries than others? Or is it that some are greater lovers of souls, more enthusiastic for the welfare and salvation of men? No doubt it is this which constitutes good mediums of spiritual influence. Are not many preachers too sweet to be wholesome, altogether ignoring the motive of fear because it is scarcely polite to mention it in our soft luxurious day? In the preface to Robertson's "Lectures on Corinthians" the editor says, "Some people were startled at the introduction of what they called 'secular subjects' into the pulpit; but the lecturer, in all his ministrations, refused to recognize the distinction so drawn. He said that the whole life of a Christian was sacred,—that common every-day duties, whether of a trade or a profession, or the minuter details of a woman's household life, were the arenas in which trial and temptation arose; and that, therefore, it became the Christian minister's duty to enter into this familiar working life with his people, and help them to understand its meaning, its trials, and its compensations." Does not the unreal distinction here alluded to between things secular and things religious prevent much of our preaching from being useful?

Ought political and public questions to be introduced, or is there not a danger of making the pulpit a "coward's castle," as there is no reply from the other side? Ought there not to be more itinerant preachers in our Church, and is it not a mistake to make every clergyman preach, whether capable or not?

Instead of forcing some to make bricks without straw, ought there not to be an authorized set of sermons to replace the old "Homilies" now out of date? Lord Lyndhurst said that it was one of the chief duties of a judge to render it disagreeable to counsel to talk nonsense. Might not bishops do something to save some of us from doing the same in the pulpit?

It is quite true that in this matter the pew is as much to blame as the pulpit. Even such a preacher as Savonarola had on a certain occasion to make a bargain with some soldiers, whom he encountered in a vessel on the river Po, and who had sought to mock him as their fellow-passenger, that they should quietly listen to him for half an hour. It is not an easy matter to get some congregations to make this bargain; but we must make every effort in our power to do so.

I.

FAINT, YET PURSUING.

"Faint, yet pursuing."—JUDGES viii. 4.

NEITHER in the Bible, nor in any other book, is there a more beautiful motto than this. It is the description given by the sacred writer to that little band of three hundred patriots who, under the leadership of Gideon, had succeeded in driving across the river Jordan the great host of the Midianites who had long been a thorn in the side and a snare unto Israel. Of these three hundred heroes, who had routed an army " like locusts for multitude," very many must have been wounded, and all were weary, but they did not give up. They were faint, yet pursuing.

There could not be a more honourable description, and it is one that is deserved by many warriors in the battle of life. That man hates the profession or business by which he earns his living. He has drifted into it or been forced into it by circumstances; but now he finds that it is uncongenial and unsuited to him. He is the round man in the square hole, and is therefore faint and weary with his life's work; but he deserves the "well done, good and faithful servant," because he does his best. A business is sometimes so laborious and monotonous that it is almost unbearable. What, for instance, is the value of life to an omnibus driver, working on weekdays and Sundays from six o'clock in the morning till twelve at night; or to the man who goes up and down so continually in a hotel lift, that he becomes part of the machine; or to women who, by working sixteen hours out of every twenty-four at needlework, can just manage to escape starvation? That half of the world which does not know how the other half lives can scarcely realize the faintness and weariness of the dim millions who work themselves to death in order to live honestly. Why does that woman, who might earn three pounds a week by a life of sin, make shirts for six shillings? Because, though faint, she has determined by the grace of God to pursue the good and the right way. Some are faint and weary with struggling against inherited disease, or tendencies to evil, but they fight their enemy to the last. Robert Collyer said: "I heard a man say that for twenty-eight years the soul within him had to stand like an unsleeping sentinel, guarding his appetite for strong drink." This recalls a glorious epitaph which was once placed on the stone above a soldier's grave—

> " Here lies a soldier whom all must applaud,
> Who fought many battles, at home and abroad ;
> But the hottest engagement he ever was in
> Was the conquest of Self in the battle of sin."

Others find that their domestic relations are incompatible with happiness; but they continue to do what is right, and to suffer without murmuring.

> " Oft in life's stillest shade reclining,
> In desolation unrepining,
> Without a hope on earth to find
> A mirror in an answering mind,
> Meek souls there are, who little dream
> Their daily strife an angel's theme,
> Or that the rod they take so calm
> Shall prove in heaven a martyr's palm."

One of these " meek souls " is reported to have said to a friend, " You know not the joy of an accepted sorrow." Of life itself many are faint and weary; but they will not leave the post where God has placed them. They do not love life; but whether their years are to be few or many, what they have to live they resolve by the grace of God to live well.

Of course when applied to brave men and women like these, the description " Faint, yet pursuing," is a most honourable one; but there are many cases where it would be anything but an expression of praise. Take the case of the selfish man. He has discovered that the result of having no high purpose in life, and of caring for no one but himself, is misery. He is seized with *ennui*, that "awful yawn which sleep cannot dispel," and is generally sick of himself through very selfishness. But though faint and weary he pursues his course still. Is there on earth a more pitiable sight than that of a man who has grown to hate some sinful indulgence which he continues to pursue merely from force of habit? At first the habit only drew him, then it dragged him, and now when it has ceased to please it hauls its faint and weary victim. "Woe unto them that draw iniquity with cords of vanity, and sin as it were with a cart rope."

But we desire to use the motto for our encouragement. Indeed it is encouragement that we want most, for on the troublesome sea of life our little bark may easily be wrecked, if courage fail and the lamp of hope burn dim. Let me describe the man that is especially in need of encouragement. He has, let us suppose, by the preaching of God's word, by the example of a friend, or more probably by reflecting on the joys and sorrows of his own life, come to be converted or changed, so that now he has his face turned toward God and goodness, instead of his back. There is at first in the change a pleasurable excitement, and the joy and peace that he gains from his newly discovered treasure are very real. But a time comes when this joy is less felt, for the simple reason that no emotion lasts long.

God gives to people, when they become religious, joyful excitement for the definite purpose of bridging over the first disagreeableness of changing habits. When there has been time for this purpose to be accomplished, a reaction sometimes sets in. Instead of joy, there is undue depression. The man begins to fancy that God has forsaken him, and that he is not making progress in the Christian life. The old habits are by no means entirely conquered, and he is rather disappointed with religion. He is faint and weary with the hard battle against his spiritual enemies. Though faint, will he go on and pursue as did Gideon's band, or will he prove a coward? Will he be of them that draw back unto perdition, or of them that have faith unto the saving of the soul?

> "Not all who seemed to fail, have failed indeed,
> Not all who fail have therefore worked in vain,
> For all our actions to many issues ead."

None of us are overcoming sin fast enough, but we must never despair. Let us take for our motto, "Faint, yet pursuing." It is only pride that tells us that we are not making the progress we ought to make. And if we do not see results, why then it is braver to continue the struggle when the tide of war is against us, than to be only able to fight when shouts of triumph are in our ears. Oh that it might be said of us in our warfare against evil passions and desires, what was said by a historian of a celebrated Cameronian regiment!—"They prayed as they fought, and fought as they prayed; they might be slain, never conquered; they were ready whenever their duty or their religion called them, with undaunted spirit and with great vivacity of mind, to encounter hardships, attempt great enterprises, despise dangers, and bravely rush to death or victory."

Many people are faint who would not be if they would only accept the invitation of their heavenly Father, and cast all their anxiety upon Him. There is a well-worn anecdote of an old woman going along a road with a heavy basket on her arm, when she was overtaken by a gentleman in a gig, who told her to get up behind him, and he would take her home. Presently, on looking round, he saw her still sitting there, holding her load in her arms. "Why do you not put down your basket when you have a chance of a rest?" he asked. "Oh, sir, it was so kind of you to carry me, I could not trouble you to carry my basket as well!" So it is that people imagine trouble, borrow it, and die before their time, because they *will* keep the basket of care in their arms.

The prophet Joel tells the weak to say, "I am strong"; and it was St. Paul's experience that when he was weak then he was strong. Our faintness and weakness, instead of hindering us from pursuing the right way, may help us to do so. As an illustration of the fact that we may become stronger by weakness, take that old story in Greek annals of a soldier under Antigonus, who had a disease, an extremely painful one, likely to bring him soon to the grave. Always first in the charge was this soldier, rushing into the hottest part of the fray. His pain prompted him to fight, that he might forget it; and he feared not death, because he knew that in any case he had not long to live. Antigonus, who greatly admired the valour of his soldier, discovering his malady, had him cured by one of the most eminent physicians of the day; but from that moment the warrior was absent from the front of the battle. He now sought his ease; for, as he remarked to his companions, he had something worth living for—health, home, and other comforts. Might not our faintness, weakness, and disappointments, like this soldier's disease, stimulate to distinguished service?

"As the bee, while making its honey, lives upon a bitter fruit, so in like manner we can never make acts of gentleness and patience, or gather the honey of the truest virtues, better than while eating the bread of bitterness and enduring hardness. And just as the best honey is that made from thyme, a small and bitter herb, so that virtue which is practised amid bitterness and lowly sorrow is the best of all virtues."

We must remember that it is not the strong and the successful, but the weary and the heavy laden, who are especially invited by Christ. "They that are whole ('strong' in the original) have no need of a physician, but they that are sick: I came not to call the righteous, but sinners." You are faint and weary in the battle against sin. Then to you the gospel message comes in two words—" Yet pursue." Give to Christ your faint-heartedness and weakness, and He will give to you courage and strength to pursue, though faint, the enemies of your soul.

II.

THORNS IN THE FLESH.

"And lest I should be exalted above measure through the abundance of the revelations, there was given to me a thorn in the flesh, the messenger of Satan to buffet me, lest I should be exalted above measure."—2 CORINTHIANS xii. 7.

IT is impossible to say what that trial was which St. Paul spoke of as a thorn in his flesh. Commentators have exhausted their ingenuity in vain attempts to discover what it was. Some think that it was bad sight, others that it was an impediment in his speech. It may have been a lingering sinful habit against which the Apostle had to contend. Perhaps it was some mental warp or a spiritual trial, such as doubt.

Certainly there are some sufferings which could not be described as thorns in the flesh. This figure seems to refer to sufferings springing from inner secret causes rather than from outward circumstances of which others have knowledge. A thorn in the flesh is a hidden cause of annoyance. Others cannot see it, for there is no apparent wound. Yet it throbs continually, taking away half our pleasure, and preventing us from giving attention to business. For instance, poverty in certain aspects might be called a thorn in the flesh. There are little secret expedients which the poor (especially those who once were better off) are obliged to have recourse to, which are very galling to a proud person. Such a thorn, too, would be a disease in the body or remorse in the mind, the consequences of excesses and mistakes in early life of which we are now ashamed.

One might describe as thorns in the flesh tormenting habits of mind, such as the habit of looking only on the dark side of things, or the habit of always looking back on the irreparable past. Many a one groans by reason of domestic incongruity and jars which are not felt in the shop and field, but which when a man turns to go home are felt, for there the thorn is. Probably all people have thorns of one kind or another in the flesh. You walk through a crowded street, and see on the faces of every one, except the very youngest, lines of suffering. You ask where are the happy ones. Each heart knows its own bitterness. No one, we say, can fully understand our case, or know where the thorn pricks. That is true, and therefore we had better show it to the Good Physician. He knows all about it, but what a relief to tell Him of it!

As we cannot discover what this thorn spoken of

by St. Paul was, let us consider the reason which he gives as to why he had it—"lest I should be exalted above measure." The Apostle had a deep spiritual nature, had obeyed the laws of Christ's kingdom, and had, as a consequence, become very learned in the deep things of God. These revelations might have exalted him above measure, and made him look down upon others as if he were porcelain and they common clay. To prevent this, he was given a humbling thorn in the flesh.

When men who, in early life, have been noted for sins of flesh and sins of blood, turn at length to God and feel within them the peace of forgiveness, they are sometimes tempted to be proud of their religious experiences, and to look down upon those who do not feel in all respects like themselves. How well it is for such persons to be given by God thorns in the flesh lest they should be exalted above measure, lest they should be infected with that worst form of pride, spiritual pride.

Perhaps no one could think much of himself if he were to steadily and lovingly examine the circumstances and characters of those with whom he meets. Almost every one has some excellency which we are without. The reason we are proud and prone to think little of others, is because we compare our excellences with their deficiencies instead of comparing our deficiencies with their excellences. Thorns in the flesh are sent to make us know ourselves as we are, and not merely as we seem.

Having now seen why St. Paul had this thorn in his flesh, let us go on to consider the way he acted under the affliction. He prayed three times for its removal, but when he found that it was the will of God that it should remain, he ceased to pray, and began to learn the lessons it was intended to teach. That is what we ought to do with our thorns. We may pray three times for their removal, but then we ought to cease, and believe that it is not most expedient for us that they should be removed.

The thorn was not removed, but the Apostle was enabled to bear it, and was taught by his heavenly Father the invincible power of weakness. "My grace is sufficient for thee: for My strength is made perfect in weakness."

Our Lord promised that if His disciples asked anything in His name it would be granted: "Ask and ye shall receive." Why then was not St. Paul's threefold prayer answered? It was answered in the highest and best sense by the gift of sufficient grace, by his being allowed to experience the power of God in him. He loved those spiritual ecstasies, with which the thorn seemed to interfere, but God showed him that it brought His presence in another and a better way. Who would dare to pray for anything unless he believed that God would answer his prayer by refusing what he asked if a refusal would be more expedient than a concession?

It has been remarked that the common idea of prayer resembles the magic ring in the Oriental tale

—as if it gave a power to man to bend the will of God. "But take as a crucial test the prayer of Christ—'Father, if it be possible, remove this cup from Me.' Here were all the requisites of true prayer—humility, perfect submission, true faith; yet the cup did not pass from Him. Either the prayer of Christ was not granted—and to assert this were blasphemy—or God grants an answer to prayer in different ways." We are not, then, to think that our prayers will get what Christ's did not, and what St. Paul's did not—what we wish; but they will obtain for us something better—what God wills. The cup of suffering will not pass away, but an angel will be sent to strengthen us; the thorn will not be removed, but grace sufficient to enable us to bear it will be given.

God's dealings with the infirmity of His apostle well illustrates the fact that His opportunity is man's necessity, that His strength is made perfect in our weakness. Man is of all created beings at once the weakest and the strongest. He is the strongest when with patience and humility he learns what God's laws are, and sacrifices his own inclinations in order to obey them. By learning and obeying God's laws in external nature men can equal the elephant in strength and the antelope in swiftness. They can draw down lightning from heaven, and with it flash messages from country to country in an instant. They can harness steam, and make it carry themselves and their merchandise all over the world. And by submitting to the laws of Christ's spiritual kingdom—to humility and self-sacrifice, man can attain to a wonderful height of spiritual knowledge and power. On the other hand, when he attempts to put his own will and ways in the place of God's, man is the weakest of all creatures.

We could all give illustrations from our own experience of the fact that a man is strong in proportion as he feels his weakness. Who has not noticed that invalids live a long time? This is because they know that they are weak, and therefore they take more care of themselves. We have all come to distrust those who boast that they are strong-willed, and that they would never yield to temptation like poor So-and-so. This is a most dangerous frame of mind, because the man who feels so strong is not likely to pray for God's help and to make use of the expedients which such a prayer might suggest. St. Paul's thorn, if in one sense it lessened his ministerial usefulness, must have given to him indirectly a thousandfold more strength by enabling him to lie like a child in the arms of his heavenly Father, and to ask Him to use him as an instrument for doing His holy will.

We learn next a lesson as to the sanctifying power of sorrow when it is taken as St. Paul did the thorn in his flesh. Suffering does not always make people better. It is like fire, and is followed by different effects according to the material upon which it falls. Fire softens iron, burns up straw, and hardens clay.

May we be enabled to take our sorrows in such a

spirit that they may soften our hearts and not harden them. May we see in our thorns blessings rather than curses. They are given to make us more humble, and force us to feel our dependence upon God.

> "Wish not, dear friends, my grief away,
> Wish me a wise and faithful heart,
> With God in all my griefs to stay,
> Nor from His loved correction start.
>
> Were it not better to lie still,
> Let Him strike home and bless the rod?
> Never so safe as when our will
> Yields undiscerned by all but God."

There is not only a reason for the existence of our affliction, but also for its degree of severity. If we are sorely dealt with, perhaps we paid no heed to lighter admonitions. "God speaketh once, yea twice, yet man perceiveth it not." That we may receive lasting benefit, it may be necessary that the lesson be written on our hearts in letters of fire. This, however, we may rely on—we shall not be taxed beyond our strength. "God is faithful, who will not suffer you to be tempted above that ye are able." And so, too, shall it be in the *duration* of our trial. When we have imbibed the teaching of the discipline—and this not unfrequently requires time, so stubborn is the heart of man—the thorn will be removed. It is interesting in this connection to notice the primary significance of the word tribulation. In Latin, *tribulatio* signifies the act of threshing. And so, as Trench tells us in his delightful book "The Study of Words": "Sorrow, distress, and adversity, being the appointed means for the separating in men of whatever in them was light, trivial, and poor, from the solid and the true, their chaff from their wheat, therefore some Latin writer of the Christian Church called these sorrows and trials, 'tribulations,' threshings, that is, of the inner spiritual man, without which there could be no fitting him for the heavenly garner." Surely this is reason enough for the existence of affliction, even were there no other, that the Christian graces in us may be matured and our faith purified.

III.

THE PERFECT WORK OF PATIENCE.

"Let patience have her perfect work, that ye may be perfect and entire, wanting nothing."—JAMES i. 4.

WE can all attain to a certain amount of proficiency at most things we attempt; but there are few who have patience to go on to perfection. Even in reference to things that we like, such as amusements and recreations, we are impatient. Most schoolboys play cricket, but the number of good cricketers is small. They all practice, but the majority wanting the patience which would enable them to practice improvingly, become worse rather than better. Practice makes perfect, but bad practice makes perfectly bad. What is wanted to make even a good cricketer is, that patience should have its perfect work. No one can be a good cricketer who does not take trouble, who is not glad to amend faulty ways of playing, who does not attend to rules.

If there is need of patience in reference even to these things, how much more do we require it in the great cricket-field of life! In the lives of almost every one there has been at some time an attempt at well-doing. It may have been "as a morning cloud, and as the dew that goeth early away," but there was at least a desire to do right, and good resolutions were made. What was wanted? Staying power. A poor widow had an only son who was the support and pride of her old age. After going on well for years, he fell in with bad companions and was led astray. Being asked to account for her son's change of life, the mother gave her explanation in these words—"I suppose he had not the gift of continuance."

"The gift of continuance"—that is what so many of us want. If genius may be described as "long patience" or "the art of taking pains," if we cannot excel at any earthly art or business without unwearily "pegging away," even so those who have done for a time the will of God have need of patience that they may receive the blessings promised to those who know how to wait. Here is the patience of the saints. Saints are those who let patience have its perfect work, who by patient continuance in well-doing seek eternal life. "Behold the husbandman waiteth for the precious fruit of the earth, being patient over it, until it receive the early and latter rain—Be ye also patient." It is only impatient children who will not give the plants in their gardens time, but pull them up to see whether the roots are growing. Men are content to have "first the blade, then the ear, then the full corn in the ear."

As a rule, the time required for the production of an effect measures the value of that effect. The things that can be developed quickly are of less value than those which require longer time. You can weed a garden or build a house in a much shorter time than you can educate a mind or build up a soul. The training of our reasoning faculties requires a longer time than the training of our hands. And moral qualities, being higher than intellectual, make an even greater demand upon the patience of their cultivator. Love, joy, peace, faith, gentleness, goodness, truthfulness—with what patient perseverance in the diligent use of God's grace are these acquired! The lower spheres of activity tax our patience less than do the higher, because it is only in the former that we can see, from hour to hour, from week to week, from month to month, or from year to year, the result of our work. "But if we hope for that which we see not, then do we with patience wait for it."

And this patience which we ought to have with ourselves, ought surely to be extended towards others —"Be patient towards all men." It need not surprise us that we cannot make others what we would like them to be, since we cannot make ourselves as we wish to be. Parents are often unreasonably impatient about the intellectual and moral development of their children. The child who has little force of character is easy to bring up. You envy a neighbour because she has no trouble with her boy. Yours may be harder to manage simply because there is more in him to be managed. It takes a great while to unfold a nature, if it be a large nature. Have patience!

Those who labour for the elevation of the masses must have that faith and patience which work where results cannot be seen. We sow expecting to reap angels, and not seeing them we are discouraged. This is not letting patience have its perfect work. How touching the lines found under the pillow of a soldier wounded in the American war—

> " I give a patient God
> My patient heart!"

Ah! if our Father were not patient, what would become of us? And, if He be so long-suffering with our great transgressions, what hinders our patience with a brother's shortcomings?

If we may say so without irreverence, we would say that we must let patience have its perfect work in our thoughts about the government of God. In our impatience we wonder why He should be so tolerant of the thorns upon which we have to tread, instead of taking them away and strewing our path with rose-leaves. God sees that these thorns are better for us than rose-leaves. "Without a combat thou canst not attain unto the crown of patience. If thou art unwilling to suffer, thou refusest to be crowned. But if thou desire to be crowned, fight manfully, endure patiently. Without labour there is no arriving at rest, nor without fighting can the victory be reached." When a storm arises, we look ahead for the clearer air and the brighter sky that will follow; and he who traces the same law in the storms of life has the clearest and truest mental vision. And when we fail to trace this law, we shall do well to patiently trust it.

> " All my life I still have found,
>   And I will forget it never;
> Every sorrow hath its bound,
>   And no cross endures for ever.
> After all the winter's snows
>   Comes sweet summer back again;
> Joy is given for all our woes,
>   Patient souls ne'er wait in vain.
> All things else have but their day,
> God's love only lasts for aye!"

The way most persons accept misfortune is the greatest misfortune of all; while nothing is a misfortune if patience be allowed to have its perfect work, as sometimes it is. In the top room of one of the houses of a miserable court, which I know well, there lives an old woman crippled and deformed in every joint by chronic rheumatism. Listen! She speaks of her gratitude. For what? Because with the assistance of a knitting-needle and her thumb, the only joint that will move, she can turn over the leaves of her Bible.

When Archbishop Leighton lost his patrimony by the failure of a merchant, he only said, " The little that was in Mr. E.'s hands hath failed me; but I shall either have no need of it, or be supplied in some other way." On his brother-in-law expressing surprise that he took the matter so patiently, he answered, "If, when the Duke of Newcastle, after losing nineteen times as much of yearly income, can dance and sing, the solid hopes of Christianity will not support us, we had better be in the other world."

"She is a living sermon," was the remark sometimes made by those who left the sick-room of one who had learned how to serve God by patient continuance in well-suffering. With her bright smiles upon us, we could not doubt that He who was Himself a Man of sorrows and acquainted with grief enables His disciples to suffer and be strong. All your ups and downs may be turned to the glory of God if you will let patience have its perfect work.

Instead of complaining, as some do, of sorrows and temptations, St. James says that you ought to rejoice to have them, "knowing that the proof of your faith worketh patience." How much patience is required to turn a deaf ear to the laughter of foolish companions, to have the courage of our opinions, to say "No" when passion or fashion call upon us to do what is wrong!

Let us remember, in conclusion, where it is that we are to get patience in the presence of temptations and sorrows. We must go in prayer, as our Master did in the Garden of Gethsemane, to the Source of all strength. If He would not go to His trial unprepared, it certainly is not safe for us to do so. If we would have patience to resist temptation, we must forecast our trial, consider what is before us, and call up resolution in God's strength to go through what we have to do. Are you going to meet people who may provoke your temper, make you talk wickedly, tempt you to spend money which you cannot afford, invite you to some form of wrong indulgence? Fight the battle on your knees before you go into the presence of the temptation. It is wonderful how patiently a man who has prepared himself by earnest prayer can conquer temptations which beforehand seemed irresistible, and bear sorrows that he had thought to be unbearable.

How poor are they who have not patience! On the other hand, as patience means self-control, or the power of restraining and moderating our desires, those who have it are perfect and entire, wanting in nothing. In the ancient times, a box on the ear given by a master to a slave meant liberty; little would the freedman care how hard was the blow. By a stroke from the sword the warrior was knighted; small matter if the monarch's hand was heavy. Even so our God gives His servants blows of trial when He desires to advance them to a higher stage of spiritual life. Jacobs become prevailing princes, but not until they have wrestled with temptations and have prevailed.

IV.

A REFUGE FOR THE DISTRESSED.

"And every one that was in distress, and every one that was in debt, and every one that was discontented, gathered themselves unto him; and he became captain over them."—1 SAMUEL xxii. 2.

WE are all familiar with the history of David at the beginning of his life when he was a shepherd-boy, and at the middle and end of his life when he became king and sweet singer of Israel; but the intervening period is often lost sight of, though it is full of interest and instruction.

At the period of which the text speaks, David was leading the life of an outcast and an outlaw. Driven from the kingdom of Israel by the jealousy of King Saul, he had fled for refuge to the court of Achish, king of Gath, Saul's enemy; but his presence soon revived the national enmity of the Philistines against their former conqueror, and he had to fly for his life.

So then, being expelled both from Israel and Philistia, nothing remained for him to do but to gather around him a band of equally unfortunate men and defend himself with his sword. Planting his standard beside one of the great limestone caves so common in that country, he summoned to the cave of Adullam all who were in distress, or in debt, or in any way discontented.

The cave was near to Bethlehem, so David was joined by his whole family, now feeling themselves insecure from Saul's fury. Besides these, outlaws from every part came to him, about four hundred men, whose past was full of disappointment and who had no hope for the future but that which was centred in their young captain. "In the vast columnar halls and arched chambers of this subterranean palace, all who had a grudge against the existing system gathered round the hero of the coming age, the unconscious materials out of which a new world was to be formed."

My brethren, cannot we see in David collecting around him all who were in distress, in debt, or for any reason discontented, a foreshadow of the Friend of publicans and sinners, of Him who said, "Come unto Me, all ye that labour and are heavy laden, and I will give you rest. Take My yoke upon you, and learn of Me, and ye shall find rest unto your souls"? Jesus Christ when on earth associated with outcasts, and spoke tenderly to those whom society counted lost. It was that feature in His character, that tender, hoping, encouraging spirit of His, which the prophet Isaiah fixed upon as characteristic: "A bruised reed will He not break."

Distress and sorrow do not always bring people to Christ. The effect of sorrow depends very much on the nature of the person on whom it falls. Instead of softening the heart and leading to God and goodness, it may make people hard, unloving, and irreligious. Nevertheless, sorrow may be and should be taken hold of as a hand stretched out by our heavenly Father Himself to draw us to Him. "Now I rejoice," St. Paul tells the Corinthians, "not that ye were made sorry, but that ye sorrowed to repentance." The Divine power of sorrow is to work repentance. By repentance is meant in Scripture change of life, alteration of habits, renewal of heart. This is the aim and meaning of all sorrow. As a maiden pierces her ears in order to hang jewels in them, so our distress is a blessing in disguise if it bring us to Christ and enable us to find the jewel of great price. Distress and sorrow —these are "counsellors that feelingly persuade me what I am," and what the world is, and that there is no rest except in the pardoning love and saving help of my Saviour. Again, a man's religion may be concealed in his heart, and may not do the good it ought to do as an example till distress come upon him and cause it to be seen in all its power. In many a true believer piety is like a drum, which nobody hears of unless it be beaten.

The cave of Adullam was a refuge for debtors, and so is the Church of Christ. We owe to God our best service of body, of mind, and of soul; but this none of us have paid or can pay. Instead of giving to Him from whom all blessings come our best service, many of us have given to Him our worst. How, then, could we stand for one moment before His judgment seat if we could not point to the perfect service of Christ, the Head and Representative of our race, our Saviour and Elder Brother? The very best of us before a jury of the meanest of men, knowing all the details, would be condemned; none could stand a jury of that sort, far less a jury of the lowest angels; and yet the worst sinner who repents and comes to Christ should not despair of standing upright in the holy place of Him in whose presence angels veil their faces, and in whose sight the heavens are not clean.

The third class of people who came to David at the cave of Adullam were those who were discontented. So, too, there is a "Divine discontent" which brings people to Christ. A man has discovered on realizing some scheme of worldly ambition that he does not enjoy his prize as he fancied he would. He has his desire, but there is leanness withal in his soul. Such an one, feeling the vanity of what he most desired, will more easily be led to Christ than one who is perfectly content with himself and his achievements. The world is unsatisfying because the soul of man is insatiable in its desires.

It is the greatness of the soul which has been made for God which renders it dissatisfied with everything less than Him.

Are you dissatisfied? Then go to Christ and fill up the hollowness of your soul with Him. God is Love and Goodness. Fill the soul with goodness and love, and you fill it with God. If we love one another, God dwelleth in us. Nothing else can satisfy.

It is well for a man when the fruit of sinful indulgence turns to ashes in his mouth, for then, if not before, he may be induced to go to Christ. The prodigal son in the parable returned to his father because he was discontented with the wages of sin. He had tried to satisfy his appetite with husks, but he found that a husk is an empty thing and by no means a substitute for food. Often as they are invited by God, some will not return until famine come to drive them back from their wanderings in the land of sin. Then is the glory of Christ's gospel seen, in becoming a refuge for those who are disappointed and dissatisfied with the pomps and vanities of this wicked world.

This is the truth which is contained in the common saying, that when people become disappointed with the world, it is the last resource to turn saint. This is often said sneeringly, and meant as a sarcasm against religion. A great preacher has answered the sneer in these words: "Let the world curl its lip if it will, when it sees through the causes of the prodigal's return. If affections crushed in early life have driven one man to God; if wrecked and ruined hopes have made another man religious; if want of success in a profession has broken the spirit; if the human life lived out too passionately has left a surfeit and a craving behind which end in seriousness; if one is brought by the sadness of widowed life, and another by the forced desolation of involuntary single life; if when the mighty famine comes into the heart, and not a husk is left, not a pleasure untried, then, and not till then, the remorseful resolve is made, 'I will arise and go to my father':—well, brethren, what then? Why this, that the history of penitence, produced as it so often is, by mere disappointment, sheds only a brighter lustre round the love of Christ, who rejoices to receive such wanderers, worthless as they are, back into His bosom."

The last thing we note about the miserable men who came for refuge to David is that they were taught by him to live good lives. They were a rough, lawless set of men, yet they could be kept in check by the influence of their beloved captain, David. Some of them at least listened to that beautiful song which he used to sing for them:

> "Come, ye children, and hearken unto me:
> I will teach you the fear of the Lord.
> What man is he that lusteth to live;
> And would fain see good days?
> Let him refrain his tongue from evil:
> And his lips that they speak no guile,
> Let him eschew evil and do good;
> Let him seek peace and pursue it."

So useful and helpful to their neighbours did these soldiers become, that the servants of Nabal could not help acknowledging as much. "But the men were very good unto us, and we were not hurt, neither missed we anything, as long as we were conversant with them."

Now surely if men's lives were made good by coming to David, the effect which coming to Christ should have upon our characters is infinitely more beneficial. If we have really come to Jesus, our friends and neighbours will observe His influence in our daily lives. We shall tell them by our patient continuance in well-doing and well-suffering that we have been with Him. The very name "Jesus" teaches us that if we really come to Him we shall be saved, not merely from the fear of punishment, but from sin.

People talk of being saved, and ask others if they are saved, and yet they seldom put to themselves this simple question—saved from what? It is too often thought that by professing certain beliefs and by feeling certain feelings we can escape the misery which it is the nature of sin to cause without giving up sin, and obtain the happiness which only comes from goodness without becoming good.

It is owing to this that religion is the sleeping partner it is in our week-day life. We fancy that so long as each Sunday we profess to have certain beliefs and feelings, we may with full hope of reward and no fear of punishment live in our professions, in our family, and in our dealings generally, as if we had never heard of a self-sacrificing Saviour.

Certainly we ought to come to Jesus in our sins, but we ought not to remain in our sins. And if we do come to Him in earnest and take Him for our Captain, He will enable us to fight and conquer those evil passions and dispositions which produce so much of our spiritual distress, debt, and discontent.

V.

MISTAKES ABOUT HAPPINESS.

"Whosoever drinketh of this water shall thirst again : but whosoever drinketh of the water that I shall give him shall never thirst ; but the water that I shall give him shall be in him a well of water springing up into everlasting life."—JOHN iv. 13.

IT is no use telling people not to seek for happiness, for to do so is a natural instinct. It is true, as Carlyle was fond of reminding us, we have no right to happiness ; nevertheless, there are, however unreasonable, in most people a hope and expectancy that if they are not happy now they one day will be. So they continue the search for happiness, and, in nine cases out of ten, fall into some of the common mistakes on the subject. One of the commonest of these mistakes is thinking that happiness depends upon things without a man, rather than upon the man within.

We do not imply that it is possible to be happy in every situation: there are certain conditions—such as slavery, extreme poverty, prolonged and severe pain—in which it would be unreasonable to expect happiness. But such circumstances as these are exceptions; and in all ordinary circumstances, if people are unhappy they ought to blame themselves rather than the outward arrangements of their lives. It is what we are, and not what we have, that constitutes our happiness.

Look at that poor, aged, broken, friendless, despised prisoner. On his back are the marks of eight scourgings; his face shows the bodily and mental suffering that he endures; he is chained night and day to brutal soldiers, who hated their prisoners because they hated the task of guarding them; he is at the mercy of an insane tyrant. This is Paul the aged, and now a prisoner of Christ; but even in these circumstances, his heart is so full of joy, that he makes the rude soldier who kept him look up with astonishment mingled with contempt, by dictating to Timothy his message to the Philippians: "Rejoice in the Lord alway, and again I say rejoice." Paul the prisoner was happier than Nero the emperor, because the man within in the first case was pure and free, while the insane fancies of Nero, "like to vermin in the nut, had fretted all to dust and bitterness."

A millionaire, upon being asked what was the happiest period of his life, promptly said, "When I was working on a farm at twelve dollars a month."

In a Chinese book it is related that a rich priest had hoarded a fine collection of jewels, to which he was constantly adding, and of which he was inordinately proud. Upon showing them to a friend, the latter feasted his eyes for some time, and on taking his leave, thanked his host for the jewels. "How!" cried the priest; "I have not given them to you! Why do you thank me?"—"Well," rejoined his friend, "I have at least had as much pleasure from seeing them as you can have, and the only difference between us that I can discover is that you have the trouble of watching them." The rich man does not enjoy more than he who has enough. He has not two mouths, so as to eat two dinners at once. He cannot drive in two carriages at the same time. "When goods increase, they are increased that eat them; and what good is there to the owners thereof, save the beholding of them with their eyes?"

There is a class of persons a key to whose character is furnished by Pope's line—"Man never is, but always to be, blest." The simple pleasures of life which it is in the power of every one to enjoy are uncared for by them. The beauties of nature on a summer-day, home—sweet home—the love of children, the pleasures of friendship: these things they will not condescend to notice, much less to appreciate at their true value. They are always expecting to be happy in a future day. They sigh for this or that place in society, and refuse to enjoy the present and daily comforts that drop thickly upon their path till that end be attained. They can never realize the fact that they are blessed in the present, and that the future will bring with it no greater blessings. Like an absent-minded man who looks about for his hat when it is on his head, they have simple pleasures near them without ever becoming aware of the fact.

Much more philosophical was the conduct of my dog "Jack." The day had been overcast; suddenly the sun shone out, and a little patch of sunshine brightened the corner of the carpet. Immediately "Jack" got up, and, with a wise look, trotted to the bright place, and laid himself in it. Let not "Jack's" example be lost upon us, but wherever there shall shine one patch of sunlight, let us enjoy it. "Heaven seems to be everywhere if we would but enter in, and yet almost nowhere, because so few can."

Those who despise the present elements of happiness that are in their power to use, and think only of some blameless, absent possible bliss in the future, are only less foolish than those are who think that happiness comes from excitement. Exciting pleasures are always followed by a reaction, and require to be administered in stronger and stronger doses. "Never seek for amusement," says Mr. Ruskin, "but be always ready to be amused. The least thing has play in it—the slightest word wit, when your hands are busy and your heart is free. But if you make the aim of your life amusement, the day will come when all the agonies of a pantomime will not bring you an honest laugh." It did not surprise Carlyle that poor women of fashion should take to opium and scandal. "The wonder is rather that these queens of the land do not some morning, struck by the hopelessness of their condition, make a general finish by simultaneous consent, and exhibit to coroners and juries the spectacle of the whole world of *ton* suspended by their garters, and freed at last from *ennui* in the most cheap and complete of all possible modes."

Bishop Butler's way of looking at life may have in it too much dyspeptic sadness, and he may not have given enough weight to the exhibition of animal spirits, but surely he was right in the main when in one of his sermons he set before his audience as their most hopeful enterprise to "endeavour chiefly to escape misery," and advised them to propose to themselves "peace and tranquillity of mind, rather than to pursue after high enjoyment." The idea of making "pleasure, and mirth, and jollity our business, and constantly hurrying after some gay amusement, some new gratification of sense and appetite," distressed him, not merely because it was a diversion from profitable thoughts and occupations, but because it was also a weariness of the flesh. The pursuit of gaiety can, he says, lead only to disappointment, bitterness, and satiety.

"Oh! if I were lucky enough to call this estate mine, I should be a happy fellow," said a young man "And then?" said a friend. "Why, then I'd pull down the old house, and build a palace, have lots of prime fellows round me, keep the best wines, and the finest horses and dogs in the country."—"And then?"—"Then I'd hunt, and ride, and smoke, and drink, and dance, and keep open house, and enjoy life gloriously."—"And then?"—"Why, then, I suppose, like other people, I should grow old, and not care so much for these things."—"And then?" "Why, then, I suppose, in the course of nature I should leave all these pleasant things—and—well, yes—die!"—"And then?"—"Oh, bother your 'thens!' I must be off." Many years after, the friend was accosted with, "God bless you! I owe my happiness to you!"—"How?"—"By two words spoken in season long ago—'And then?'"

God has made us for Himself, and we cannot rest except in Him. All things under the sun must appear vanity of vanities, or emptiness of emptiness— "hollow" as the *blasé* used-up man now calls them— when we attempt to quench with anything less than the highest good, the highest truth, and the highest beauty, souls "athirst for God, yea, even for the living God."

The Preacher, not without bitter experience, came to the conclusion that the chief good—indeed, the only good—for man is to fear God and to keep His commandments. If at any time we should feel unhappy, let us review our principles and our practice, and see if the fault be not rather within than without, and remember that, by whatever name we may seek happiness—whether pleasure, honour, power, or wealth—we shall seek her quite in vain, except under the familiar and too often repulsive name of—Duty.

Man only becomes happy when, ceasing to think of self, his one desire is to serve God. Self is the shadow that darkens the lives of so many. Empty yourself of self, and God will fill you. Empty yourself of God, and then you will lose your life by trying to save it. We should attend to the moral of the Book of Ecclesiastes, which is this: that selfishness is a great mistake, and produces no fruit of real happiness. And does not a greater than Solomon assure us that " Whosoever drinketh of this water shall thirst again: but whosoever drinketh of the water that I shall give him shall never thirst; but the water that I shall give him shall be in him a well of water springing up into everlasting life"?

Truly religious people are happy because they do not think of themselves. Having food and raiment here they are content, for their treasure is in heaven. They are cheerful because they serve God. Even in great tribulation they can rejoice in Him, having learned in whatsoever state they are therewith to be content. "I am sure," said General Gordon, "the secret of true happiness is to be content with what actually we have; and," he added, "we raise our own goblins." "Man walketh in a vain shadow, and disquieteth himself in vain: he heapeth up riches, and cannot tell who shall gather them. And now, Lord, what is my hope: truly my hope is even in Thee." Amen.

VI.

A WISE CHOICE.

"And the speech pleased the Lord, that Solomon had asked this thing."—1 KINGS iii. 10.

THERE are around the city of Chester high walls, on the top of which runs a much-frequented path which is reached by a flight of steps. It is said by the people of the place that whatever you wish for when standing on these stairs you will get it in a year's time, and so they are called the "wishing stairs." What would each of us now wish for if we were on these steps? Perhaps we would find it more difficult than we think to select that for which we should wish; for though we are discontented enough, yet when we come to ask ourselves: "What is it exactly that I most desire?" we are often at a loss to know.

It was not so with Solomon. He did not find it difficult to answer when asked what he most wanted. In Gibeon God appeared to him in a dream, and asked him to make whatever request he pleased Solomon did not ask for the things that most men consider of the greatest value. He did not ask for riches, nor honours, nor a long life, nor to be able to conquer enemies, but for an understanding heart to discern between good and evil. " And God said unto him, Because thou hast asked this thing, and hast not asked for thyself long life; neither hast asked riches for thyself, nor hast asked the life of thine enemies; but hast asked for thyself understanding to discern judgment; behold! I have done according to thy word; lo! I have given thee a wise and an understanding heart; so that there hath been none like thee before thee, neither after thee shall any arise like unto thee. And I have also given thee that which thou hast not asked, both riches and honour, so that there shall not be any among kings like unto thee, all thy days." Suppose, now, that each of us were asked by God to make whatever request we pleased—for what would we ask? Would we ask for what is best, or for something far inferior? If one of us were to pray to God, not merely for what we think we ought to pray for, but for what, in our heart of hearts, we most desire, what kind of prayers would we utter, or, rather, breathe?—for I fancy we would be ashamed to speak them out. Any one who could overhear these prayers would learn our real characters. Some of us would pray for more money; others, perhaps, for beauty, or a commanding presence; others to have certain titles added on to our names; others to have unlimited desires and unlimited means of gratifying them; others to have old age postponed; others to have the supposed pride of their enemies abated. How many would ask for wisdom, for understanding to discern between good and evil, for a sensitive conscience in good working order? Most men would even prefer a conscience that would fall asleep and so give them peace; but Solomon asked for the opposite of this for two reasons. First, because he was humble; secondly, because he felt the responsibility of his position. He was humble, for he said, "I am but a little child; I know not how to go out or come in." And what are any of us in this strange, unintelligible world but children, who cannot go a step forward or backward without falling, unless we are supported by the grace of God?

Again, Solomon prayed for an understanding heart, to discern good from evil, because he felt the responsibility of his position. He knew that without God's guiding spirit he could not rule so great a people. If *we* do not feel the same need of an understanding heart, may it not be because we refuse to look our responsibilities in the face? We are not kings nor judges nor anything great; nevertheless, we all have responsibilities. If for nothing else, we are all responsible to God for the management of the life He has given us. For every one it is a serious thing to be alive; but for him who does not ask for, and who does not care to have, an understanding heart, life is a curse and not a blessing by any means. Then there are always other lives that depend upon us, more or less. Surely parents must feel the responsibility of having to bring up children in an age when it is difficult to do it well. Poor Margaret Fuller, recording in her diary the birth of her child, expressed a feeling of responsibility with which many parents can sympathize: "I am the mother of an immortal being? God be merciful to me a sinner!"

But what exactly is this understanding heart for which Solomon prayed? It is that wonderful thing which is so much spoken of in the Bible under the name of Wisdom. It is goodness or the fear of the Lord, the opposite of godless wickedness, which is "folly." In the eighth chapter of the Book of Proverbs, Wisdom is described as coming into the high places of the streets, and crying as a town crier at the gates of cities to all whom she met praying them to take hold of her, and to show her forth in their lives. It has always been the teaching of the Church that Wisdom is only another name for Jesus Christ, the Word of God, or the expression of the wisdom of God. If this be so, then what Solomon really prayed for, though he did not know it, was that this mind might be in him which was in Jesus Christ—the spirit of wisdom and understanding, the spirit of counsel and might, the spirit of knowledge and of the fear of the Lord.

Solomon's choice was a wise one, and God was pleased with it, and gave him the inferior things which he might have asked for, but did not—such as long life, riches, conquest over his enemies. Just so it is that those who ask for and receive the Spirit of Christ have all other things added. They get long life, even eternal life; for "this is life eternal, to know Thee, the only God, and Jesus Christ, whom Thou hast sent." "He that hath the Son hath life"—that spiritual, heavenly life whereby we live to God and enjoy peace with Him. And this life which comes from Jesus Christ, is a long one, even in this world, and even if He who lives it seem to die comparatively young; for a life worthily spent ought not to be measured by years, but by deeds.

> "We live in deeds, not years; in thoughts, not breaths,
> In feelings, not in figures on a dial.
> We should count time by heart-throbs. He most lives
> Who thinks most, feels the noblest, acts the best."

Again, those who ask for and receive God's Holy Spirit get also the highest kind of riches. They are content, and he who is most contented is the richest of men. They have no hungry appetites and greedy ambitions; for they learn from their Master, Jesus Christ, that "sweet reasonableness" which moderates and controls them. They do not envy, but rather pity, the great and rich, who have their good things in this world, but neither part nor lot in the kingdom of heaven. For themselves, they see the King in His beauty, and are satisfied. "He that loveth silver shall not be satisfied with silver;" but "My people shall be satisfied with My goodness, saith the Lord." The soul fixed upon eternal glories finds earthly things reduced to their true diminutive proportions, as the climber of some lofty mountain sees from its eminences lakes below reduced to the size of little pools, plantations to patches of grass, and men to pygmies.

The third thing which it is said that Solomon might have asked for, and which he received because he did not ask for it, was the power to conquer his enemies. Is not the conquest of enemies the privilege of the true followers of Jesus Christ? They conquer their enemies by kindness, and heap coals of fire on their heads by returning good for evil, blessing for cursing. That the influence of a true Christian is a conquering force, we have all seen in the career of him about whom so much has lately been written. All agree that the great personal influence of General Gordon was gained, not in any military academy, but in the school of Christ. We know, too, how rich he was in being able to despise and refuse riches, and how honourable in caring nothing for honours.

Perhaps it may be said that nearly all people do desire an understanding heart, and that they need not be urged to make the choice. Yes, they desire it; but they cannot be said to choose it. There is a difference between desiring and choosing. There are many young people who, if you asked: "Do you choose to be educated?" would answer: "Certainly; I do choose to be educated." But, no; they do not. They desire to be educated; but there are myriads of desires that never ripen into a choice, as there are a million blossoms and comparatively few apples. When those who desired to be educated saw that a choice would involve self-denial and drudgery, they preferred to put it off till to-morrow, or next week, or next month, or next year, and to take the consequences.

A young man desires to be rich; but as soon as he finds that gaining wealth requires self-denial, painstaking industry, and integrity, he does not choose riches. He chooses self-indulgence; he chooses pleasures; he chooses companionship; he chooses the present and lets the future take care of itself. Men desire to have an honourable character and the happiness that comes from well-doing. They desire it; but whether they choose it or not, we can only tell when we see how they act. If they are circumspect, vigilant, and self-denying; if they take a high standard; if they steadily press their way up and buffet every temptation, then we say that they have chosen to have a high character. Otherwise we say that they have merely desired it. A fool can desire; but it is a wise man that chooses. In the same way many persons desire to obey Christ, and hope that one day they shall do so. They say: "I respect religion more than riches or worldly honours or anything else." But do they choose to have in them the mind of Christ or an understanding heart to discern between good and evil? Are they willing to take the steps that it is necessary to take? Are they willing to put forth the exertions that must be put forth in order to be true Christians? It is easy to desire, it is difficult to choose, and this is the explanation of the religious sentiment which produces little or no result in life. People in church are carried up by singing, by prayer, by the present effect of preaching to a point which looks as though it would culminate in piety, and then they go home and are as those who see their faces in a mirror and forget what manner of men they are. We make one more remark, and that is that the power of desire increases and the power of choosing decreases in a wicked life. It is the reverse in a holy life. The power of turning desires into choices increases as a man advances in the Christian life. Whatever he desires within the bounds of possibility he can get and keep. In the case of men who live away from God the opposite takes place. There desires augment, but their power to choose diminishes, so that in the end they become reprobate or incapable of reformation. May we be enabled to choose Wisdom, for our choice, though brief, is yet endless!

VII.

THE DAY OF SALVATION.

"And they told him that Jesus of Nazareth passeth by."—
LUKE xviii. 37.

THE scene brought before us is a very touching one. A blind beggar is shown sitting at the entrance of the town of Jericho. According to St. Mark, his name was Bartimeus the son of Timeus. Hearing the hum of many voices and the tramp of a multitude of people, he asks for an explanation of the crowd, and learns that they follow the great miracle-worker of Nazareth, Jesus Christ. Unable himself to see Him, the poor blind man has to learn that the great Healer is not merely near, but is actually passing by, from those who, less indifferent and unfeeling than the rest of the crowd, attend to and reply to his questions.

When we are in some lonely out-of-the-way place, where news is not easily obtained, we are very ready

to complain of its dulness; but what must it be to
be blind, to live on this earth without ever having
seen it, to have no idea of form and colour, to have
knowledge and wisdom at one entrance quite shut
out.

Do we thank God for sight, we who know that the
light is sweet and that it is a pleasant thing for the
eyes to behold the sun? The power of seeing is one
of those common blessings which we are wont to
despise because they are common, than which
nothing is more unreasonable and ungrateful. The
fact that we share a blessing with millions of our
fellow creatures, ought surely to make us value it
more rather than less. When we meet a blind person in the street, perhaps we look at him as if his case
were peculiar; but, considering what a wonderful
instrument the eye is, and how easily it may go
wrong, the wonder is not that here and there an
individual should be blind, but that any one should
see.

The blind must lead a lonely life, for we who see
cannot fully sympathize with them; but by a kind
of instinct this poor Bartimeus seems to have felt
that One was passing by who would feel for him as
no one before ever did, so he cries out and asks Him
to have mercy upon him. The unfeeling crowd rebuke
and try to silence him. "Do you think," they probably said to him, "that the Great Teacher has
nothing to do but to stop and listen to you, a beggar,
who are always asking for something? Let Him

pass on and us with Him. He is busily engaged and cannot attend to you." But Bartimeus was not one of those who miss blessings for want of a little perseverance. He had in him that energy of character, or violence, to use the strong expression of our Lord, which takes the kingdom of heaven by force. So the only attention he gave to the rebuffs and insults of the people, who had no compassion for him, was to cry all the louder to Him whom he heard of as being eyes to the blind and feet to the lame. "Thou son of David, have mercy on me. And Jesus stood and commanded him to be brought unto Him; and when he was come near He asked him, What wilt thou that I should do unto thee? And he said, Lord, that I may receive my sight. And Jesus said unto him, receive thy sight; thy faith hath made thee whole. And immediately he received his sight, and followed Him, glorifying God; and all the people when they saw it gave praise unto God." Thus it was that Bartimeus was enabled to glorify God and received himself the thing he most longed for, because he had in him the persevering energy of true faith.

And now, brethren, let us think of some of the lessons the record of this miracle has for us. We in one sense are all more or less blind. We may see with our bodily eyes, but the eyes of our souls are holden so that we do not see into that other world which is not less, but more real than this one, though it can only be seen by faith or the eye of the soul.

God, heaven, our own souls, how blind we are to these realities, and how much need there is for us to cry unto Jesus that He would help our unbelief and give to us spiritual sight. At times, no doubt, we do feel in need of the Great Healer. We desire more light, and cry unto him to have mercy upon our condition of darkness. Then the frivolous and profane do their best to laugh and rebuke us out of these strange gloomy thoughts, as they call them. They would have us hold our peace even though the Saviour may be passing by. This we must not do. The more they rebuke us, the more must we persevere in crying for mercy, and a time will come when Jesus will have us brought unto Himself, it may be by the hand of affliction, it may be through disappointment with the wages of sin—by some means we shall be brought to Him, and have our eyes opened that we may behold wondrous things out of His law.

"Jesus of Nazareth passeth by." He does so at every crisis and change in our lives. He passes by in the short but most critical time of youth, when passions are strong and little experience of the pitfalls to be guarded against in life has as yet been obtained. When weakness, sickness, and old age are exchanged for the health and brightness of youth, again He passes by. In all time of our tribulation; in all time of our wealth; in the hour of death, and in the day of judgment, He is near at hand; but, blind ourselves, we cannot see Him, and we have not the faith of Bartimeus who believed those who could see Him, and when He was passing by perseveringly cried unto Him for mercy.

But the consequences of ignoring the fact that a merciful Saviour is near to us are very serious. If the young do not recognize Christ when He is passing by, they will probably commit sins that will waste their strength and make then prematurely old. If in time of health we are not urged by the felt nearness of Jesus to consecrate our health to His service, we run a great risk of losing it through folly and wickedness. As people do not recognize that Christ passeth near to them when they are in health, even so they do not see as they ought His hand in their sickness. An invalid lamented to a lady who came to see her, that she had abused her health before it was taken from her. The friend replied, "I hope that now you will take care not to abuse your sickness." Assuredly we abuse our sickness when we do not see the hand of God in it, and do not allow Jesus of Nazareth, who passeth by our bed, to bring us nearer to Himself. And how could we, with hope and good courage, walk through the valley of the shadow of death without His rod and His staff to comfort us?

What Jesus, who is now passing by, is to our sinful, sorrowful race, has been beautifully expressed by an old poet in the following lines:

"Christ is a path, if any be misled,
He is a robe if any naked be;

> If any chance to hunger He is bread,
>   If any be a bondman He is free.
>
> If any should be weak, how strong is He!
>   To dead men life He is, to sick men health,
>   To blind men sight, and to the needy wealth,
>   A pleasure without loss, a treasure without stealth."

How blind to our interests are we if, when One who is all this passeth by, we do not regard Him or ask Him to help us. "Jesus of Nazareth passeth by," but it will not be so always. These words may one day be changed into "Jesus of Nazareth *has* passed by." The alteration of the words is a slight one, but oh, what a terrible difference there is in meaning! Jesus of Nazareth has passed by, the time of grace is gone and nothing remains but judgment.

There are in the history of every life what has been called the Three Times—a time of grace, a time of blindness, and a time of judgment. In the time of grace, Jesus passes by and gives us every opportunity of taking Him for our Master and Saviour. If this time be neglected, there follows a time of blindness and indifference. Jesus will not always trouble us by knocking at the door of our hearts. He will, if a deaf ear be too long turned towards Him, take His Holy Spirit from us and pass by. "Ephraim hath turned to his idols, let him alone." God's method of punishing us is to make us punish ourselves.

If, when the Saviour passes by, we say that we will not have this man to reign over us, then He gives us up to our own heart's lusts, and what these are we find from bitter experience, not saviours certainly, but the most cruel of tyrants and tormentors. The worst punishment that can befall a man is to become blind and indifferent to Jesus of Nazareth when He is passing by, until it is too late and He has passed.

After that the judgment. We shall be judged for every opportunity we ever had of hearing and knowing that Jesus was passing by. Every means of grace that was in our power to use, and which if it had been used would have brought us to Him, is noted down in God's book of remembrance, and we shall have to give an account if we ignore or neglect it. To-day, then, if you hear His voice harden not your hearts. While Jesus of Nazareth is still passing, and before He has quite passed, let us ask Him to have mercy upon us and enable the eyes of our souls to receive sight.

Friends and companions may think our prayers for light and salvation unnecessary. They may laugh at us for being peculiar, and rebuke us for differing in opinions and practice from themselves; but if we really value that for which we seek as Bartimeus did, we shall not soon be discouraged. The more others rebuke, the more a great deal shall we cry "Jesus, thou son of David, have mercy upon me." "My son, stand steadily, and put thy trust in Me; for what are words but words? Do thou give diligent ear to My word, and thou shalt not care for ten thousand words spoken by men." Do not fear the frown of the world. When a blind man comes against you in the street, you are not angry at him; you say he is blind, poor man, or he would not have hurt me. So you may say of those who rebuke you for crying unto Jesus or doing anything else you know to be right—they are blind.

If in this way we perseveringly cry unto Jesus for spiritual sight, undaunted by the rebukes of the careless, and those who are enemies to peace, our eyes shall be opened, and we shall see the King in His beauty, and the heavenly mansions that are prepared for those who unfeignedly love Him. This will cause ourselves and all our true friends to give glory, praise and worship, unto God.

VIII.

SISERA NO MATCH FOR THE STARS.

" They fought from heaven ; the stars in their courses fought against Sisera."—JUDGES v. 20.

BEARING in mind that " the kingdom of God is not meat and drink, but righteousness, and peace, and joy in the Holy Ghost," we may say that all things, even the stars in their courses, fight against every one who, like Sisera, puts himself in opposition to the plans of the Ruler of the universe. If you co-operate with, and act according to the laws of God, then you will in the long run prove victorious ; if you do not, why then these laws will crush you. They are stronger than you. Sisera was no match for the stars in their courses. God never leaves Himself without a witness in the hearts of men, and there is a certain amount of truth in every religion which has in any degree satisfied numbers of men. Now the truth which seems to have been the life and soul of the religion of Mahomet, and which enabled it to spread so widely and rapidly, was just this which we are now considering. That the stars in their courses, representing the laws of God revealed in nature, are against every one who does not resign himself to God, who, instead of saying, "Not my will but Thine be done," says, "Not Thy will but *mine* be done!" Mahomet's two watchwords were, "Allah Akbar," "God is great;" and "Islam," "Submit." And is not this resignation to God above all things commanded by Christianity? Did not the Author and Finisher of our faith utter these words—the sublimest "Islam" or submission ever spoken—"Father, if Thou be willing, remove this cup from Me: nevertheless, not My will but Thine be done"?

The difference between a truly great man and a small man is this: The great and true man cannot put up with what is not real and genuine. He struggles to know things as they *are*, not as they *seem*. His whole soul revolts from shams and make-believes. His word is true, his work is thorough. He conforms himself to God's laws, and, therefore, though he may not succeed at first, and may be despised and persecuted by those who cannot understand him, still, all nature and nature's God are on his side: the stars in their courses fight for him, and he goes on conquering and to conquer. Certainly Luther only spoke the truth when he said to his judges, "It is neither safe nor prudent to do aught against conscience."

But it may be asked, " Do we not hear many false men praised and called ' respectable,' while true men are often suspected and cast out as evil ? Is not the share of this world's goods which falls to the lot of really good people as often as not very small ? Is it not safer, therefore, to make the best of *both* worlds—that is to say, to serve God when it is not inconvenient, and when it is to serve man ?" No ! it is not safer, for " God is not mocked, and whatsoever a man soweth, that shall he also reap."

Just exactly according to the kind of seed we sow shall be our harvest. If a tradesman cheat, but cheat prudently—if he tell lies, but " lies like truth," he has sown the seed of worldly success ; and, if he be cunning enough not to be detected, and content himself with that amount of dishonesty which " the public " can tolerate, he will become rich. Do you, an honest, truthful man of business, envy him ? Do you complain that your honesty is a hindrance to your success, while custom pours into the doors of your less scrupulous neighbours ? Then you should consider the price they have paid for their success—unclean consciences and inward dishonour. Sow the seed of such men, and you will reap their harvest. Cheat, lie, be unscrupulous in your assertions, and custom will come to you. But if the price be too dear, let them have their harvest, and take yours. Yours is a clean conscience, a pure mind, an honesty and nobleness which can look man in the face and hold communion with God. Will you exchange that harvest for theirs? Then why do you complain? God is not going to give such a poor reward as £ s. d. to honesty, honour, and truthfulness. If you sincerely love and serve Him; if, like Moses, you esteem "the reproach of Christ greater riches than the treasures of Egypt," then you may be poor and despised. For God does not pay His true servants with the coin of worldly success, but with purity of heart, likeness to Himself, and a crown of righteousness.

A man is powerful or powerless, just in proportion as he submits to God's laws. And, first, to speak of physical laws, or those relating to matter. It is by obeying nature that we learn her secrets. We cannot enter into the kingdom of nature any more than into the kingdom of grace, except as a little child. A medical man in the kingdom of nature cures or kills, just in proportion as he has carefully or carelessly studied the laws of health, and obeys them. Perceiving that our bodily afflictions are contrary to the will of God, and therefore curable, he sets himself manfully to work in the light of God, and by the help of God to discover and correct the errors that produced them. By studying and making use of the physical laws of God's universe, we can improve health and prolong life. We can send messages with lightning speed, and make changes in the world such as the steam engine has caused.

On the other hand, there is no favourite of nature who can be intemperate, and not suffer from ill-health, or live near bad drainage and escape fever. No matter how intellectual or even religious you may be, if you hold your hand in the fire it will certainly be burned. A Christian is as liable to losses in his business if he do not conform to the laws of commerce, on which wealth depends, as an atheist is. The wind will wreck a shipful of missionaries if she be not well sailed and piloted, just as much as a ship manned by pirates. Transgress God's physical laws, and even the stars in their courses fight against you. Just so there are spiritual and moral laws, by compliance with which we receive blessings, and which, if not obeyed, are as ready as the stars to fight against us. Such laws are these: "If we love one another, God dwelleth in us." Let a man in his every-day domestic and public life be selfish, exacting, hard, unkind, and his punishment is that he will never be able to really love God or to believe that God loves him. Another such law is that without living up to the faith we already have, we cannot increase our faith or receive any answer to the question, "What is truth?" "If any man will do His will, he shall know of the doctrine."

It is our highest duty and wisdom to resign ourselves to God, and the religion of the Cross should teach us that "silence and sorrow are strong," and that "patient endurance is God-like." Our Christianity, if it be of the right kind, will teach us to care for and think little of our own happiness either here or hereafter, but very much of serving God; to give ear to no vain sorrows and wishes; to know that we know nothing; that the worst and cruellest to our eyes is not what it seems; that we have to receive whatsoever befalls us as sent from God, and say, " It is good and wise, God is great ! " " Though He slay me, yet will I trust him."

Whether we like it or not, we must submit to God, but to those who really believe in a God of love as revealed by Christ's cross, such submission is comparatively easy. Those who do not believe in a God at all, or who, like most heathen nations, believe in revengeful malignant deities, are *forced*, as we all are, to submit to nature's stern laws, which are the laws of God. But to submit when we cannot help submitting is one thing; to do so willingly, believing that infinite love guides and orders all things, is quite another.

As the stars in their courses by submitting to God do His will, and fight against all who do it not, so let us willingly submit and work together with God. Let us pray that ours may be that true Christianity which can say, " Not my will, but Thine be done," that the same trustful spirit may dwell in us as that which inspired the resigned words of St. Paul, " For the which cause I also suffer these things: nevertheless, I am not ashamed; for I know whom I have believed, and am persuaded that He is able to keep that which I have committed unto Him against that day."

Man, it would seem, of all created things, has alone

the terrible privilege of breaking the laws of his Maker. Hence he may sink below a brute, or rise in glory above the stars in their courses. And this makes the thought that we do not obey God's laws as readily as do even things without life a very sad one. It may be that when staying by the seaside my hearers have at some time been led into such reflections on a summer evening when they contemplated the sea with its darkness smiled upon by the lights of heaven. Then, perhaps, as they thought of their own lives at the suggestion of sea and sky, they learned from "the stars in their courses" this lesson—

"'And once more,' I cried, 'ye stars, ye waters,
   On my heart your mighty charm renew;
Still, still let me, as I gaze upon you,
   Feel my soul becoming vast like you.'

From the intense, clear, star-sown vault of Heaven,
   Over the lit sea's unquiet way,
Through the rustling night-air came the answer—
   'Wouldst thou be as these are?—*live* as they.'"

We do not sufficiently realize to ourselves how everything in the world is sustained and carried on by God. We speak of "laws of nature" and "secondary causes," while we forget nature's Lawgiver and the Cause of causes. We believe that He created the world, and at different periods performed miracles; but we can scarcely be said to believe that our every-day work, our joy, our pain, and everything else, comes from Him with whom we have to do.

We see God's hand in what is extraordinary; we do not see it, as we ought, in things ordinary and common. We believe that God worked miracles in the first century; we forget that every good and useful work of the nineteenth is from Him. Yet surely, as long as we are thus unbelieving, miracles have been wrought for us in vain. We have not learned the lesson they teach. For "a miracle is the outward manifestation of the power of God in order that we may believe in the power of God in things that are invisible. Miracles were no concession to that infidel spirit which taints our modern Christianity, and which cannot believe in God's presence except it can see Him in the super-natural." Rather they were to make us feel that all is marvellous, all wonderful, all pervaded with the Divine Presence, and that the simplest occurrences of life are miracles.

Without God we can do nothing. His Spirit guides more churches than our own, has inspired and does inspire in some degree other books than our Bible, is the giver of every good and perfect gift, is not far from any one of us. Let us conduct ourselves in every relation and occupation of life as if we believed we were what we *are*—" workers together with God "—and all things must work together for good. Let us put ourselves in opposition to Him, and all things, even the stars in their courses, shall fight against us.

There are few people who exactly like their life's business and position. Well, let us remember that we are called into the position of life in which we are by God Himself, and that if our work be not noble, it is for us to ennoble it by doing it in a noble spirit. "Art thou called being a servant? Care not for it." The poor domestic servant who does her work thoroughly and honestly, "not with eye-service, as a man-pleaser, but as the servant of Christ, doing the will of God from the heart," is as high in God's sight as the Prime Minister of England who does his work equally well, and higher if she do her work better. Then there are some whose life is one long disease by reason of weakly constitutions, and to whom the toil of daily life and the anxious discharge of duty under adverse circumstances is pain and grief. Who say in the morning, as they despair of getting through their day's work, "Would God it were even!" and at even, when a long wakeful night is before them, "Would God it were morning!" And what is our hope? Truly our hope is even in Thee! Christ crucified *placarded* (Galatians iii. 1) before our weary eyes reminds us that, no matter what the cross may be which we are given to carry, our sorrow and misery are not for ever; that this world is not a playground, but a school, in which we are all being educated for the higher duties and employments which shall be entrusted to us in the next. That he who bravely and thoroughly in this unintelligible world does his obscure and commonplace work in the midst of difficulties, and with only a rushlight to guide his steps, shall have glorious and noble work to do in that better world where the bright shining of the Son of Righteousness shall enable us to see how all the sorrows, trials, and difficulties which we have here are not worthy to be compared with the glory that shall be revealed hereafter. People should consider that where God's laws are every moment being transgressed by others, even though they themselves are innocent, misery must fall to their lot. God's kingdom is not yet come, therefore His will is not now done on earth as it is in heaven. And this transgression of God's laws by most men causes even those who do His will unhappiness, and must do so until His kingdom come —that is a kingdom in which nothing but His will shall be done. "Then shall the righteous shine forth as the sun in the kingdom of their Father."

IX.

THE BABYLONIAN CAPTIVITY.

"They that carried us away captive required of us a song."
PSALM cxxxii. 3.

TO the mocking invitation of their conquerors "to sing something"—some spirited patriotic strain, forsooth!—the poor captive Israelites, who were in no singing humour, could only answer with their tears. The Babylonians, enjoying as they did "cornet, flute, harp, sackbut, psaltery, dulcimer, and all kinds of music," desired for a change to hear their new subjects performing what they called "the Lord's song." But the exiles were not going to waste *that* on a foreign land. As for those harps that had lately shed the soul of music through the long-drawn aisles of the temple at Jerusalem, they would hang them up in sullen silence on the branching poplars and tamarisks (not "willows," as these trees are not found in Babylonia) that grew along the canals of the Euphrates, rather than play them for the amusement of men who had destroyed the capital of their country and the temple of their God.

Certainly it was to no mean city that Nebuchadnezzar transported or caused to migrate ($\mu\epsilon\tau o\iota\kappa\epsilon\sigma\iota a$ is the word used by Greek writers) the children of Israel in the year 587 B.C. When we think how large London is now, and see it extending on all sides every day, we can scarcely realize the fact that our modern Babylon is little more than a village as compared with "the glory of the Chaldee's excellency," the Babylon in which Israel was imprisoned for about seventy years. If the imperceptible circumference of our modern capitals has exceeded the limits of Babylon, yet none in ancient times or modern can be compared with its definite enclosure, which was on the lowest computation forty, on the highest sixty, miles round. Who has not heard of the "hanging gardens of Babylon"? We are told that forests, parks, gardens, were intermingled with the houses—suburbs, as it were, in the centre of a metropolis. The city walls, entered by one hundred gates of brass, were 300 feet high, or nearly equal in height to the tower of Westminster Palace or to the dome of St. Paul's, and along their summit ran a road which admitted of chariots with four horses turning on it. The great palace of the king was itself a city within a city, seven miles round, and its gardens, expressly built to convey to a Median princess some reminiscence of her native mountains, rose one above another to a height of more than seventy feet, on which stood forest trees side by side with flowering shrubs. Pining for the courts of the Lord's house, certainly the sight was but poor consolation to the new comers. Still, they could now behold the great temple of Bel, the largest edifice that ever was or ever has been (not excepting the great temple in Egyptian Thebes, the Byzantian St. Sophia, or St. Peter's at Rome) consecrated to worship. It rose to the height of 600 feet, and its base was the same number of feet square. Its several stages were black, orange, crimson, gold, brilliant blue, and silver. And the inner life of Babylon was quite in keeping with its outward show, and must have seemed to the exiles, as to subsequent ages, a type of "the world" itself. Nebuchadnezzar's cavalry and chariots, of which both Ezekiel (xxvi. 7; xxiii. 24) and Jeremiah (iv. 13) speak, were to be seen careering through the streets, "his chariots as a whirlwind; his horses swifter than eagles." Before the eye of the Israelite captive there passed daily what would have seemed to him a lively procession had he been in better spirits— "Captains and rulers clothed most gorgeously, all of them desirable young men, horsemen riding upon horses girded with girdles upon their loins, exceeding in dyed attire upon their heads, all of them princes to look to, after the manner of the Babylonians of Chaldea."

Were the Israelites desirous of mental improvement? They had now an opportunity of indulging

their taste, for science both true and false made
Babylon her home. Magicians, astrologers, and
sorcerers abounded in Chaldea, "where the entire
celestial hemisphere is continually visible to every
eye, and where the clear, transparent atmosphere
shows night after night the heavens gemmed with
countless stars of undimmed brilliancy."

Nor could the captives accuse their masters of
ill-using them. They were comparatively few in
number. A large part of the lower classes were left
in Palestine, and those who were transported consisted
chiefly of the princes, nobles, and priests, with the
addition of artizans in wood and iron. Of these
many, like Daniel and the three children, rose to
positions of honour in the land of the stranger, and
Jeremiah even advised acquiescence in their expatri-
ation—"Build ye houses, and dwell in them; and
plant gardens, and eat the fruit of them; take ye
wifes, and beget sons and daughters; and take wives
for your sons, and give your daughters to husbands,
that they may bear sons and daughters; that ye may
be increased there, and not diminished. And seek ye
the peace of the city whither I have caused you to be
carried away captives, and pray unto the Lord for it;
for in the peace thereof shall ye have peace."

Nevertheless, the exiles had good reason for adding
their tears to the waters of Babylon. However
grand their new place of residence might be, it was
not *home*, and that made a sad difference to them.
Though they made the best of it, they could not

conceal from themselves the fact that they were stripped bare—for that is the meaning of "guloth," the Hebrew word for "the captivity." They were stripped bare of country, of sanctuary, and even of their God, if at least they were to listen to the conqueror's mocking question, "Where is now thy God?" Human sorrow has never found so loud, so plaintive, and so long-protracted a wail as that of those for whom Ezekiel, Jeremiah, and the writers of the captivity psalms became mouthpieces. No other period is so likely to have produced that "prayer of the afflicted (Psalm cii.), when he is overwhelmed, and poureth out his complaint before the Lord," when the nation, or at least its most oppressed citizens, could compare themselves only to the slowly-dying brand on the deserted hearth, or to the pelican standing by the desert pool, pensively leaning its bill against its breast, or to the moping owl haunting some desolate ruin, or to the solitary sparrow, pouring forth its melancholy note on the housetop, apart from its fellows, or to the ever-lengthening shadow of the evening, or to the blade of grass withered by the scorching sun. There were the insults of the oppressors; there were the bitter tears which dropped into their daily beverage, the ashes which mingled with their daily bread; there was the tenacious remembrance which clung to the very stones and dust of their native city. Remorse, too, must have added to the sorrow of the captives, for they could not but remember that "they were haughty, and committed abomination before God; therefore He took them away, as He saw good." When "fulness of bread and abundance of idleness" was in Israel, she weakened herself by luxury and dissipation, and, as a consequence, she was unable to resist the invader. Of this remorse would now remind her.

But the moral gold of the exiles was to be refined from dross by their fiery trial. In their case we discover an exception to Bacon's saying, that "Prosperity is the blessing of the Old Testament, and adversity of the New," for the blessings that came to the captives out of their adversity were neither few nor trifling. Judea, seated not beneath her native palm, but beneath the poplars of the Euphrates, began now for the first time to desire One who should take her infirmities, and bear her sicknesses, rather than the Messiah of glory she had looked for in better days. Now she sought for a Messiah who, while doing no sin Himself, would suffer with sinners, to proclaim liberty to the captives, and the opening of the prison of sin to them that are bound; to sanctify their sorrows.

I. When she lived in Palestine, Israel could never be altogether restrained from coquetting, so to speak, with the idolatry of the nations that surrounded her. But the very extravagance of the Babylonian worship that now came under her notice would make her ask herself, " Have I been quite free from this polluting idolatry? Has there not been a lie in my own right hand, and, if so, ought I not to go for refuge now with greater trust than ever before to the one good and true God?" "It seemed as though the identification of Polytheism with the odious thought of the Babylonian exile and oppression had *destroyed its spell*, even as the fires of Smithfield disenchanted the English people of the charm of the Roman Church, and turned them into zealous adherents of the Reformation."

II. With the conviction that they that wait on the one true God shall renew their strength, there sprang up in the exiles *a strong sense of individual responsibility*. They felt with Ezekiel that "the soul that doeth righteously shall live, and the soul that sinneth it shall die." Hence such examples of moral courage as Daniel in the lions' den, and the three children who were not careful to answer Nebuchadnezzar, choosing quietly to burn—if need be—rather than worship the golden image he had set up. "How many an independent patriot or unpopular reformer has been nerved by their words to resist the unreasonable commands of king or priest! How many a little boy at school has been strengthened by them for the effort when he has knelt down by his bedside for the first time to say his prayers in the presence of indifferent or scoffing companions!"

III. Daniel strengthened himself for his trial with prayer, and it is to be noted how the captivity in this matter of prayer as well as in other matters *deepened the spirituality of the nation*. To this result the very destruction of the "holy and beautiful house" at

Jerusalem, where their fathers praised the Eternal, was favourable. The absence of any ritual or local form threw the exiles back on their own hearts and consciences, to hold communion with Him who had declared by the overthrow of His earthly sanctuary that "Heaven is His throne," and His favourite dwelling-place with "the contrite and humble spirit" of man. And hence it is that from the captivity dates, not indeed the first use, but the continued and frequent use of prayer "as a potent instrument for sustaining the nobler part of man as the chief access to the Invisible Divinity." The spiritual sacrifice of praise and thanksgiving, which was a reasonable service, took now the place of the less reasonable morning and evening sacrifices of bulls and goats.

IV. Another beneficial result of the captivity was the widening of Israel's views as regards the Fatherhood of God. "Neither let the son of the stranger, that hath joined himself to the Lord, speak, saying, The Lord hath utterly separated me from His people." These words of Isaiah express the more charitable and more reasonable opinions that would be suggested to the exiles by contact with foreigners in reference to the moral government of Him who hateth nothing that He has made, who is the Father not of the Jews only, but of all flesh.

In such ways as these the exiles were enabled by the grace of God, "to lead captivity captive"—to "find in loss a gain to match," even the gain of having become more like Him who heard the affliction of His people, and thus spoke of them to His servant Isaiah, " Comfort ye, comfort ye My people. Speak ye comfortably to Jerusalem, and cry unto her, that her warfare is accomplished, that her iniquity is pardoned ; for she hath received of the Lord's hand double of all her sins." Nations, as well as individuals, are in this way allowed by God to leave the past behind them, and to start afresh in the race of duty. But what are the lessons taught to us by the history of the Babylonian captivity ? Certainly there are many men and women to whom the 137th Psalm will be full of a touching significance if they look back on the time when they first found themselves *alone in London.* A young man, after being brought up with loving care in the country, is sent with a Book of the Lord's songs packed by his mother in his trunk to serve his time at some business in our modern Babylon. Will he not be ready to shed tears on his first Sundays spent in town when he thinks of friends at home singing one of the songs of Zion, in which he can no longer join, deterred perhaps by the ridicule or want of sympathy of strangers ? And the very desire of others that he should " keep up his spirits " and be a " jolly fellow "—such jarring requests will only increase his heaviness. What should such a young man do ? Let him, before his better feelings grow cold, resolve rather to forget the cunning of his hand if he be an artizan, or the cunning of his business faculty if he be in a merchant's or lawyer's office ; let him resolve to forget these or never to acquire them at all rather than to forget the love of his home and the worship of his *mother's* God—in one word, Jerusalem. It is sad to think how many there are who seem to act on a resolution the reverse of that formed by the mourners in Babylon. They acquire cunning of hand or a money-making head, and prevent themselves forgetting their cunning by assiduous practice; but what of their old homes and the religious lessons learned in them—what of Jerusalem? This, perhaps, they have almost forgotten. When travelling abroad, did Englishmen remember Jerusalem, and prefer her above their chief joy, they would realize the presence of One who could dispel the loneliness of a strange land, and deliver them from the many temptations of friendlessness.

Again, there are many generous souls whose best impulses are imprisoned by circumstances over which they have no control. Round men have got into square holes, and find no scope for the best energies of their nature. Children long to help their parents; but they are far from home, or their desire is in captivity, by reason of poverty, ill-health, or anything else. Parents cannot do all they desire for their children. Let these, and all who find themselves in adverse circumstances, think of Israel weeping on the banks of the Euphrates—let them think of how she waited patiently on the Lord in poverty, in humiliation, in a strange land, full of sin and scoffing; and of how He delivered her from Babylon in His own good time, as of old He delivered the same Israel out of bondage in Egypt. Whatever the nature of our captivity may be, we should remember for our comfort that—

> " Stone walls do not a prison make,
>   Nor iron bars a cage ;
> Minds innocent and quiet take
>   That for an hermitage ;
> If I have freedom in my love [to Christ],
>   And in my soul am free [from sin]
> Angels alone that soar above
>   Enjoy such liberty."

X.

EJACULATORY PRAYER.

"So I prayed to the God of heaven."—NEHEMIAH ii. 4.

THE circumstances which called forth this prayer of Nehemiah enable us to see of what kind the prayer must have been. No prayer could have been used on the occasion except one that might be described as an instantaneous instinctive thinking to God.

Let me recall to your memories the way Nehemiah was situated when he used this prayer. The seventy years of the captivity had expired, and many of the Jews had returned to their own country under the guidance of Zerrubbabel. Nehemiah was not one of those who returned. He had prospered and acquired a place of high honour in the country of those who had conquered the Jews and carried them into captivity. He had become cup-bearer or chief butler to Artaxerxes, king of Persia. But though Nehemiah had himself prospered, he was not selfish enough to forget his poor countrymen who had returned to Jerusalem. One day as he was in the palace at Shushan, he heard sad news about his brethren. He learned that the remnant that were left of the captivity were "in great affliction and reproach," that the wall of Jerusalem was broken down and the gates thereof burned with fire.

Hearing this, Nehemiah is greatly troubled. He prays to God for his countrymen, and he resolves to help them himself by bringing their case before the king and asking him to assist them. It was some time before he had an opportunity of doing so, but at last an opportunity did present itself. One day as Nehemiah was giving a cup of wine to the king, Artaxerxes remarked that his face was very sad: "Wherefore the king said unto me, Why is thy countenance sad, seeing thou art not sick? this is nothing else but sorrow of heart. Then I was very sore afraid." He was sore afraid. It might have cost him his head this crime of looking sad before the majesty of an Eastern tyrant. Besides, Nehemiah was very anxious to enlist the services of the king on behalf of his countrymen. He knew that bad advocacy may spoil the best cause, and this would make him nervous, so he prays to God. But how does he do it? Picture to yourselves the scene. Artaxerxes the king is sitting in his royal state, probably at some great banquet, and beside him sits his wife. Nehemiah has been asked why he is sad. There is only one instant in which he can make reply, and neither time nor place for going down on his knees and making a formal prayer. Fast as lightning he thinks to God, and from that instinctive instantaneous prayer he gains enough strength and courage to plead with tact and wisdom the cause of his countrymen, and to gain from the king leave to return to his country to help them.

Here, then, brethren, is an instance of what may be called instantaneous, instinctive ejaculatory prayer, just the sort of prayer that we ought to acquire a habit of in this age of business and haste. If our spiritual life is not to be starved out of us, we must pray. Just as surely as our bodies cannot live without food, our souls cannot live without prayer. When we say that a man lives a Christian life, we mean that he lives in communion with the Source and Fountain of that life—that is to say, that he is ready to think to Christ in doubt, in trouble, in temptation.

But the prayer that feeds the soul is something far different from a mere form. Forms may be necessary, or at least of use, in public worship; but when alone and in private, out of the abundance of the heart the mouth speaketh.

Some say that they do not know in what words they should pray to God. Any words will do, or no words. If there are songs without words, surely there may be prayers without words. A working man once came to Rowland Hill telling him that he was in great distress, that all his things were to be sold, and that he could not work because his tools were in pawn. Rowland Hill told him that if the loan of five pounds would help him out of his difficulties, he would lend it on one condition. The man was delighted, and said he would do anything he asked him. "Well, then," said Hill, "you must ask a blessing on the way you intend to spend the money. If you do not do this you will probably squander it, and I do not feel justified in lending it to you." "But," said the man, "I never did say a prayer, and I cannot do so now." Being told by Rowland Hill very firmly that he could not have the money without a prayer, the man went down upon his knees and said, "O Lord, I thank Thee and I thank Mr. Hill for the money, and I pray Thee to enable me to make a good use of it." "Get up," said Rowland Hill, "that is as good a prayer as you could possibly pray, for it is straight from the heart;" and he lent him the money. Any words will do if only they are really felt; for in addressing God the greatest eloquence is foolishness, and worse than that if it is not sincere.

Any place, too, will do—or perhaps we should rather say that a person ought not to go into a place where he could not pray. In some of the most crowded thoroughfares of London, I often have noticed people as I passed them moving their lips though they were quite alone. Were they speaking to God? Probably some of them were as they went on their way to scenes of temptation and of distress, or to where they would have to encounter difficulties or answer perplexing questions. There is no reason why a prayer thought to God even in a London street should not be as earnest as any spoken aloud in the grandest cathedral.

Nor does prayer necessarily need time. That the busiest may pray not only in the sense that to labour is to pray, but in the meaning usually given to the word, is testified to by the following letter which was lately addressed by a poor woman to the editor of the *Banner of Faith*.

SIR,—Having read in the *Banner of Faith* that bit about "Where to pray," I feel I should like to tell your readers my experience on the subject, and I shall be very thankful if, by God's blessing, it does some good to others.

Poor women with large families often think they have little time for prayer or praise. As I am a poor woman with a large family, and know the value of prayer and praise, I will tell them how I find time for it. Whilst I am cleaning the house I lift my heart to God and say, "Create in me a clean heart, O God, and renew a right spirit within me, for Christ's sake. Amen." When I am washing the clothes I say, "Wash me in Thy Blood, O Jesus; Wash me and I shall be whiter than snow." Then as I get to each of my children's clothes I pray for them separately, not aloud, but in my heart. Again, if I pick up the shirt of one who drinks, I ask God to change his heart, to show him his state in God's sight, and to help him to give up drink and become a sober, godly youth. If I am washing the shirt of another who has a horrid temper, that is a terror to us all, I pray to God to break his stubborn temper, to soften his heart of stone, and give him a heart of flesh. If I am washing anything belonging to a girl who is idle, then I pray God to show her her sin, and change her whole nature, by the Holy Spirit. Yes, I pray for each as I know their need.

Then when I am sewing, I find lots of time both for prayer and praise.

When I light or mend the fire, I say in my heart, "Kindle, O Lord, a sacred fire in this cold heart of mine." Even in nursing we can pray. If all around is confusion, and wrangling, and misery, we can pray for patience to bear every ill thus put upon us. Though our hearts may be made sore, yea, may feel ready to break by ill treatment from those we love and are working hard for, yet, if we continually pray for them, we may be sure God will answer our prayers in His own time. God is everywhere, near, very close to every needy soul : we cannot see Him, but we can feel Him near, yea, nearer to us than our own families, who are crowding round us. All we want is faith.

Let those who feel the want of time or place for

prayer try my experience, asking God continually to increase their faith, and I am sure they will feel no difficulty as to " where to pray."

Yours in Christ,
EXCUSE MY NAME.

Of course there are special times and places set apart for prayer, and it is our duty to use them; but when this cannot be done, any time, and any place, and any words will furnish one who is in vital union with his Redeemer means of communicating with Him. What more unfavourable time for praying than the moment after being asked a perplexing question? What place could be less adapted for prayer than the immediate presence of a king and queen? Yet it was at this time and in this place that Nehemiah prayed to the God of heaven, just because it was then and there that he wanted His help.

Let us, then, for our own comfort and safety, acquire Nehemiah's habit of ejaculatory prayer. We say habit, for if he had not been accustomed to thinking to God in calm circumstances, he could not have done it when flurried and alarmed at the king's question. Temptation may be presented when we are least expecting it; quicker than electricity could carry the message thought may wing a prayer to heaven, " Keep, oh, keep me from yielding to this temptation." No unexpected peril, no unthought of difficulty, can surprise us at any place or any moment when we cannot follow the example of Nehemiah, and "pray to the God of heaven."

> " Prayer is the soul's sincere desire,
>   Uttered or unexpressed,
> The motion of a hidden fire
>   That trembles in the breast.
>
> Oh, Thou by whom we come to God,
>   The life, the truth, the way ;
> The path of prayer, Thyself hast trod,
>   Lord, teach us how to pray."

XI.

GOD'S METHOD OF PUNISHMENT.

"Therefore shall they eat of the fruit of their own way, and be filled with their own devices."—PROVERBS i. 31.

IN many passages of the Bible, as well as in the history of the world and of our own lives, we find that God's usual way of punishing us is to let us punish ourselves. In this way man is led by bitter experience to see his own folly and God's wisdom. We might purchase wisdom cheaply if we would obey the still small voice of God speaking in our hearts; but since we hate knowledge and do not choose the fear of the Lord, in order to show us our folly God takes away His despised counsel and reproof from us, and lets us eat the fruit of our own way and be filled with our own devices. In the text this terrible condemnation is pronounced against Israel: "But My people would not hearken to My voice, and Israel would none of Me: so I gave them up unto their own hearts' lust: and they walked in their own counsels." In another passage it is said that when lust came upon Israel in the wilderness and they tempted God in the desert, that then "He gave them their desire: and sent leanness withal into their soul." To punish the people for worshipping the golden calf, "God turned, and gave them up to worship the host of heaven." For rebellious Ephraim there was no other punishment than to be let severely alone: "they be blind leaders of the blind. And if the blind lead the blind, both shall fall into the ditch."

In the Epistle to the Romans St. Paul describes the punishment that was inflicted on the sinful heathen world in these words: "And even as they did not like to retain God in their knowledge, God gave them over to a reprobate mind (a mind void of judgment), to do those things which are not convenient."

> "We, ignorant of ourselves,
> Beg often our own harms, which the wise powers
> Deny us for our good ; so find we profit
> By losing of our prayers."

That is the way God treats His obedient children, but when we will not be guided by Him He grants all our wishes and desires to show us how foolish and miserable they are. When a man is "cursed with every granted prayer," he learns by bitter experience that it is possible to be his own worst enemy. He has got enough rope, and he proceeds to hang himself with it. He has plenty of opportunity to sow to the flesh if he wishes to do so, and the natural consequence of this sort of sowing is a harvest of corruption. His long-indulged desires become tyrannical tormentors. He derives no pleasure from indulgence, but he cannot do without it. Suppose a man cares for nothing else than making money, he is pretty sure to to succeed in doing so; for as the late Mr. Vanderbilt used to say, "There is no secret about amassing wealth; all you have to do is to attend to business and go ahead, except one thing, and that is never tell what you are going to do until you have done it." By this sort of prudence he will become rich, but if he is hard, selfish, and unloving, what good will his millions do him? What is money if the power of enjoyment is lost, and how can a man be said to be rich if the higher and better part of his nature is impoverished? The man is filled with his own devices, and finds them very unsatisfying.

St. Mark tells us that in Nazareth our Lord could do no mighty work because of the unbelief of the people. This shows us how our sins defeat the gracious purposes of God towards us, how we hinder Him, in a manner, from doing what He wishes to do for our good; how we make it impossible for Him to avoid punishing us, although He has no pleasure at all in the death of the wicked, but rather that he should turn from his sins and live.

God sent His Son into the world to die for us; but there are some who make Him to have died for them in vain. Instead of taking Him for their Saviour and obeying Him as their King, they will eat the fruit of their own way and be filled with their own devices. Jesus wept over Jerusalem, and desired to gather her children together under His protection, to save them from themselves and from the wrath to come. He would, but they would not; and the rebellious will of man is thus said to have disappointed and turned aside the gracious will of God. It is in this manner that the promises of God are to be understood as conditional; He will give us good things if we will do our part; not if we neglect it or do the contrary to it. Certainly if God wished to turn men into machines, He could overrule every heart that it should desire and do nothing but what was agreeable to His will. But instead of doing this, He has given to us the dignity of freedom which involves the terrible possibility of disobeying His commands.

To the thoughtless and careless it seems the best thing for them to be let alone by God. "What have we to do with Thee, Jesus, thou Son of God? art Thou come hither to torment us before the time?" This is the cry of devil-possessed men, proud of their liberty, and not wishing any restraint to be put upon their actions. Those, however, who think back seriously on the history of their lives, can trace most of their errors to the fact that they have tried to take themselves, so to speak, away from the guidance of God. They know that it would have been much happier for them if they had allowed themselves to be wound up like a clock and made to go right. Bitter experience may have taught some of us as it did Lord Byron, that for a man to be "lord of himself" is to have an "heritage of woe." If so, let us arise and go to our Father, and ask Him no longer to leave us to ourselves as a punishment for our waywardness; but to guide us into the good and the right way.

> "I was not ever thus, nor prayed that Thou
>   Shouldst lead me on;
> I loved to choose and see my path; but now
>   Lead Thou me on.
> I loved the garish day, and spite of fears,
> Pride ruled my will: remember not past years."

What is the condition of the lost? Is it not one in which the capacity for good has been extinguished by their own fault? They have "done despite unto the Spirit of grace," and "their consciences (are) seared with a hot iron," so that they cannot repent, not because an arbitrary decree prevents them from doing what they would wish, but because they have no wish to repent.

> "The deaf may hear the Saviour's voice,
> The fettered tongue its chain may break;
> But the deaf heart, the dumb by choice,
> The laggard soul that will not wake,

> The guilt that scorns to be forgiven;—
> These baffle e'en the spells of Heaven."

"Evil men and seducers," we are told, "shall wax worse and worse, deceiving and being deceived." Having refused to retain God in their knowledge, they can but go further and further in the direction in which they have set their wills; "He that is filthy, let him be filthy still." The condition of the lost is represented to us in Scripture as akin to that of the devils: "Depart from me, ye cursed, into everlasting fire, prepared for the devil and his angels."

> "No God is there; no Christ; for He
>   Whose word on earth was Come,
> Hath said Depart! go, lost one, go,
> Reap the sad harvest thou didst sow;
> Join yon lost angels in their woe;
>   Their prison is thy home."

"Thy home," because thou hast unfitted thyself for any better home.

Within the man who delights in sin and loves darkness rather than light, there is a hell of his own making from which he cannot depart any more than from himself. In the awful words of Cardinal Newman: "If we wished to imagine a punishment for an unholy, reprobate soul, we perhaps could not fancy a greater, than to summon it to heaven. Heaven would be hell to an irreligious man. He would find no discourse but that which he had shunned on earth, no pursuits but those he had disliked or despised, nothing which bound him to aught else in the universe and made him feel at home, nothing which he could enter into and rest upon." People may laugh at a hell consisting in pools of fire and brimstone; but they cannot deny the truth of what this imagery is meant to teach. If they are thoughtful and serious they cannot deny the awful reality of the hell which is made by sin, and which cannot but separate the unrepentant sinner from God. That hell will be essentially connected with the past lives of the sufferers, its torment being, not an arbitrary punishment inflicted by God's will, but what we have prepared for ourselves by our sins in this life. "The unholy soul," says Leighton, "like the mystical Babylon, makes itself a cage of unclean birds, and a habitation of filthy spirits; and if it continues to be such, it must, when it dislodges, take up its habitation with cursed spirits for ever in utter darkness." That first instinctive hiding of Adam from the face of God among the trees of the garden, is everlastingly repeated by every sin-conscious soul. Shame, fear, hate, drive the man further and further away into the darkness where he thinks and hopes God is not. Men go on ever crying to God, "Let us alone;" "Depart from us;" "Only let us get away from Thee somewhere—anywhere;" till at last this prayer is granted, their freedom is allowed them, they eat of the fruit of their own way, and are filled with their own devices.

We believe, however, that it is only those who are beyond reformation and who have altogether decided for the devil, that God in this way leaves alone to be creatures of their own appetites and the prey of their sins. Those who have not forfeited His love by continuing in evil and sinning against the light, He chasteneth. He does not let them alone, but inflicts sharp discipline upon them, in order to make them like Himself. When a man is sinking down under the influence of intense cold or narcotic poison into a deadly sleep, his only chance of life depends upon the mercifully merciless, persistent teasing, worrying of his friends. The poor diseased animal goes away alone to die, and will die if man, with his skill, does not follow and hunt and force with knife or drug. The sorrow-stricken mother will sit paralyzed, cold and hard, by her dead darling, till some wise meddler can find a key to open the fountain of her tears, and save her from death or madness.

"Purge me with hyssop and I shall be clean." We want God not to let us alone, but to take hold of us and to discipline us, in order to make us like Himself. A child would feel much pained if his father said that in future he would have nothing more to do with him, and would never check him or save him in any way from his folly. In our weakness we beg hard to be let alone, and it is not for sinners to speak harshly of such feelings. Nevertheless, God's best servants have always desired any severity that might cleanse them from past stains, deter from soft yielding in the future, and burn into their innermost being a hatred of sin.

XII.

OUR FATHER'S CHASTISEMENT.

"Purge me with hyssop, and I shall be clean."—PSALM li. 7.

THESE words of David echo the deepest longing of the human heart.

It is true, that often, perhaps generally, our weakness desires nothing so much as to escape punishment. All would be well, we fancy, if only the consequences of our sins could be prevented from following them.

In a word, we wish far more to be saved from punishment than to be saved from sin.

Nevertheless, in our better moments, we desire to be made clean even by the hyssop of punishment. We would never be fully satisfied if our sins were merely pardoned while we ourselves should remain for ever as we are—no better, no purer, no truer, no nobler.

Of all prayers, this one of David is the last we should have expected him to utter under the circumstances. He had just perpetrated the greatest sin of his life. Yet he does not pray to be saved from the punishment of his crime against Uriah; but to be made clean from the stain of it, even by means of the hyssop of suffering. Nor was he saved from the punishment of his sin. Bathsheba's child dies, and it was this affliction which caused David to see the sinfulness of his own heart, to repent of his crime, to become reconciled to God.

Very different from David's prayer for purification is the common cry, "Oh, save me from punishment, make me comfortable and happy; but as for sin, I don't much care to be saved from that."

A soft luxurious age dreads suffering much more than it dreads sin. Even into the so-called "religious" world has our selfishness entered. While there is a great deal of anxiety about salvation from punishment, there is far too little hatred of sin *as such*.

Now, these feelings must greatly influence our conception of God's character. If we believe that suffering, even purifying suffering, is the worst thing that can happen to us, we shall begin to fancy that the God of love would never inflict it upon us. On the other hand, if we recognize the truth that sin is a far greater calamity than suffering, we shall pray that God in His great loving kindness would give us victory over ourselves and purify us somehow, if by no other means then by sharp suffering.

Too frequently we degrade by weak sentimentality those words, the meaning of which we shall never in this life quite spell out—"God is love." If the characteristics of even good men are not in fact separated from each other, should we think of God's attributes as separable? Can there be perfect love without perfect justice? No, nor is that true mercy which rests on weakness and indifference to the eternal distinction between right and wrong, rather than on love and perfect goodness.

Amongst men there are three sorts of friendship or love. There are those who value their friends only because they are instrumental in giving pleasure and comfort to themselves. They relieve them from troublesome thoughts, and satisfy that instinct for society which man as a social animal feels. Of course this sadly common sort of friendship is little more than another name for selfishness. There is again another kind of love which is by no means evil, and yet quite different from the highest. It is the friendship of those who are ever seeking to give pleasure to their friends and to make them comfortable, but who do not try to make them better. This is good as far as it goes, for we are entrusted with the happiness of each other.

Nevertheless by how much is it better to be good than to be comfortable, by so much is he a truer friend who thinks more of improving the object of his love than of giving pleasure. The advice of such a one will always be good, though not always agreeable. He will never give present pleasure to be followed by future degradation. False, indeed, is that love which puts the lower above the higher, and drags down what it loves by pandering to desires inconsistent with honour and duty.

Nay, more, human love must sometimes inflict positive suffering, " must be cruel only to be kind." Parents must correct their children. Friends are false to friendship if they do not discountenance when necessary, even by painful expedients, what is wrong in their friends.

Of course this highest kind of love is that alone which is to be attributed to God. How false, then, is the whispered notion that those whom the Lord loveth, he chasteneth *not!* What *is* inconsistent with the love of a Father, is that He should let His children quite alone. If God were unloving, He would let us alone, and care little whether we are good or bad, pure or impure, selfish or unselfish. If He were like some lazy, indifferent earthly fathers, He would not take hold of us, as He does, and discipline us, in order to make us like Himself. He would leave us to be mere creatures of our appetites, the sport of our own whims, the victims on whose vitals our besetting sins are to prey for ever and ever. Take away that severity which purges with hyssop, and we cannot realize God's love for us, because then He would not wish us to become clean.

And so it is that those who, like David, have felt this, did not pray to be saved from punishment, but the reverse. In our weakness we beg hard to be let alone, and it is not for sinners to speak harshly of such feelings. Nevertheless, God's best servants have always desired any severity that might cleanse them from past stains, deter from soft yielding in the future, and burn into their innermost being a hatred of sin. " Happy is the man whom God correcteth," says Job. To Israel Moses announces, "That as a man chasteneth his son, so the Lord thy God chasteneth thee."

In what has been said, God's punishments both here and hereafter are supposed to be of a reformatory character. Does the spirit of Christ prompt men now-a-days, to devise plans by which prisoners shall be made better, and not worse ; and shall God's chastisements make sinners worse instead of better? Dante and the schoolmen, and thousands of really charitable men, were and are of the opinion that all hope is lost to those who enter God's place, or as it should be called *state*, of punishment.

The question can only be tried by the touchstone which is supplied by the spirit of Christ's gospel, and the letter of His word rightly translated and interpreted according to time, place, and circumstances. To an increasing number of good Christians this spirit and letter appear at least to suggest that God's fiery punishments are cleansing fires, not kindled in vengeance, but for our own sakes, in order to purify us. Secondly, that His punishments shall be adequate, neither in excess nor defect ; and lastly, that they shall be inflicted according to the capacity and opportunities of the offender. Whatever allowance can possibly be made for our weakness, for our ignorance, for the impediments to holiness which we have inherited, for those which the circumstances of our lives have created—all this shall certainly be made. We know who is to be our judge. The man Christ Jesus—He who was tempted like as we are, and who is therefore touched with the feeling of our infirmities.

All this we say, not out of feeble sentimentality, the very thing against which this sermon is directed, but because there is great danger in teaching doctrines such as men's hearts cannot believe. Tell people that God is going to inflict monstrous punishments, and they will rush into the opposite error, and fancy that He is not going to punish at all. Now, beside the immoral laxity of such a thought, we have tried to show that it degrades our conception of God's love, and also that of our own sonship; for "what son is he whom the father chasteneth not?"

In the case of every man, sin is degradation, though we may not know it now, and degradation is misery —misery which shall only cease when sin, and the remembrance of it, shall cease. Goodness and deepest joy, badness and deepest misery, will, in the long run, be seen and felt to be inseparable. Just because God loves sinners, and hates sin, He has made a necessary connexion between sin and misery, happiness and goodness, so that, until we are purified, we cannot be happy.

Serious people cannot help asking themselves at times, "Are the generality of men good enough for the popular fixed heaven, or bad enough for a fixed hell." Certainly there are few so good, that in the fulness of time they could not be made better. God Himself only knows what He will do with those for whom men cease to hope. It may be, that through sphere after sphere of reformatory punishment, step after step, age after age, we shall all have to pass, until we become what God would have us be—until the results of Christ's great love shall be fully realized in that hour to which the apostle looked forward when he said, "And when all things shall be subdued unto Him, then shall the Son also be subject unto Him that put all things under Him, that God may be all in all."

Let us then pray with our hearts, and earnestly strive to be delivered from evil. Delivered we must be, every one of us, before we can be happy, for God has so arranged His universe, that we cannot be saved from the penalties of sin without being saved from sin itself. Only let us understand the true nature of sin's penalties, as they are seen by the light of our Saviour's cross. They are not signs of wrath, but of a righteous government in the world—a Father's loving discipline, intended to make His children like Himself.

XIII.

CHRISTIAN FRIENDSHIP.

"Then they that feared the Lord spake often one to another: and the Lord harkened and heard it, and a book of remembrance was written before Him for them that feared the Lord, and that thought upon His name."—MALACHI iii. 16.

THESE are the words of Malachi, who was the last of the Old Testament prophets. He lived about four hundred years before the birth of our Lord. During these four centuries no prophet appeared, and there was no open vision or manifest revelation. To the majority of the nation of Israel God seemed to have utterly forsaken His people, and few believed Malachi as he faithfully proclaimed God's intention of sending a Messenger, a Refiner, a Purifier in the person of the Messiah, who was to fulfil the prophecies of the last and of all previous prophets.

And this prevailing unbelief was the cause, as it

always is, of widespread wickedness. Malachi's picture of his time is a dark one. Priests and people were so bad that it was useless to expect those blessings which had been promised as the reward of faithful obedience. Had God cast them off utterly, and was there nothing to be hoped from trying to serve Him? Many of them did not scruple to say that it was so. "It is vain to serve God; and what profit is it that we have kept His ordinance, and that we have walked mournfully before the Lord of hosts?"

Nevertheless a remnant was left. A few did believe in the coming of Christ and lived in preparation for the Refiner's fire. And what were the means which by God's grace enabled them to resist the temptations of an unbelieving and wicked generation? How were they strengthened who fought the better fight, and "maintained against revolted multitudes the cause of truth"? By holy friendship. Knowing that union is strength in religious as well as in secular things, they formed close friendships one with another and often spoke together of their hopes and fears—"Then they that feared the Lord spake often one to another: and the Lord hearkened and heard it, and a book of remembrance was written before Him for them that feared the Lord, and that thought upon His name. And they shall be mine, saith the Lord of hosts, in that day when I make up my jewels."

God in His providence has appointed many helps

for those who desire to serve Him and to lead good lives, but of these none is so important as the influence of good friends. Strange that some should be as careless as they are in a matter which has such important effects upon them! They would not willingly keep bad horses or bad dogs, why should they be less particular in choosing their friends?

Youth is, above all other periods of life, the time for making friends, the friendships then formed being the closest and most lasting. In forming these friendships, young people would do well to remember that the friendship of the bad, or of those who never try to live at all above their world, is enmity against God. We must not follow the multitude to do evil, nor be anxious to be popular with every one. "Woe unto you when all men speak well of you." He who makes friends of those who in heart and mind are entirely unlike God, cannot have God for a friend.

Another rule is not to choose friends on a low principle and from a low motive. Too many do this. They desire to have for friends those who entertain them, who flatter, who make the time speed more quickly, who give low pleasure, rather than those who would help them in the culture of conduct and character.

The best definition of a friend is "He who makes you do what you can." He who induces you to make the most of yourself, who, so far from leading you into temptation, endeavours to guard you from it, such an one is your best friend. And we are to remember that it is not so much by the words they speak or by outward and apparently important actions as by silent, unconscious influence that friends help every moment to mar or make our characters. A party of seamen believed they had gained sixty knots one day in their course, but it was proved by observation they had lost more than thirty; the ship had been urged forward by the wind but driven back by an undercurrent. How many undercurrents of trivial actions, or even looks and manners, influences scarcely heeded, may be hindering our Christian progress! On the other hand, God may be using the example of a friend, who little knows it, to bring us to Heaven. Angell James traced his solemn impressions to the consistent life of a lad with whom he was thrown into companionship; they shared the same bedroom, and he was greatly influenced by the regularity with which his friend was wont to pray and read the Bible. That companion, leading his quiet Christian life, little dreamed that he was stirring thoughts and feelings that would inspire congregations at home and abroad, for the spoken and written words of Angell James have had a large amount of influence.

Our Lord did not so much enjoin it as take it for granted that His followers would always strengthen and encourage each other by praying and speaking together. "Where two or three are gathered together" there He promised to be, and He told them that if two of them should agree on earth as touching anything that they should ask, it would be done for them. When He sent forth His seventy disciples during His own earthly life to preach the gospel through the cities of Judah, He sent them forth two and two together. So again, after His resurrection, the apostles were seldom without a companion on their different journeys. Paul was accompanied either by Barnabas, or afterwards by Silas, or Timotheus, or Luke. What the apostles needed in their journeys as preachers of the gospel, we need equally on our journey through life. Indeed, the great object for which Christians were formed into a church or society, was that they might afford to one another mutual comfort and support.

"They that feared the Lord spake often one to another." We can imagine what their conversations were about. They would speak of the temptations that beset them in their particular spheres of life, and the best way of resisting them. There would be always a cheerful, hopeful word for the downcast. They would not boast and publicly give thanks that they were better than others, but as little would they be hypocrites of the devil and be ashamed of the little good that was in them. If one of these God-fearing people saw another doing something which was unworthy of his profession, he would not scruple to give him a word of kindly caution. He would remember the command, "Thou shalt in any wise rebuke thy brother, and not suffer sin upon him."

Certainly they that fear the Lord are bound to avoid that self-righteousness which, if we were not watchful, might lead us to form a sort of Mutual Admiration Society, but we are equally bound to form a Mutual Improvement Society.

Christ says, "If thy brother sin against thee, go and tell him his fault between thee and him alone: if he hear thee, thou hast gained thy brother." Thou hast *gained* thy brother; and so far as you have been thinking most for him and least for yourself, shall the unsought blessing stream down upon you most abundantly from the Throne on high; and at your own sorest need shall you receive that mercy that blesseth him that gives and him that takes. But suppose your brother has not sinned against you, but against himself or against another, what then? Ought you to allow the sin to increase more and more because it would require a sacrifice of distaste and shyness to speak to him about it?

Those who are Christians in earnest gradually lead one another on to higher views of life and duty; a knowledge of their mutual faults make them unreserved to each other; they are not afraid of saying all that is in their hearts; they make known to each other their particular difficulties and temptations; they feel that they are engaged in the same struggle; and each is often able to give assistance to the other on one point, whilst by others he may himself require to be aided in his turn.

Those, then, who fear God and who have given

their hearts to Christ, ought often to speak to each other in order to encourage the workings of the Holy Spirit within them. Compelled as they often are to become to them who are without the law, almost as if they were without the law; obliged to hear so often in silence the expression of those low principles which are on a level with the minds of worldly men; they should themselves in time be tainted by the common infection, if they had no like-minded friend with whom they could speak, and from whom they could receive an answer in a kindred spirit. Therefore every God-fearing man for the sake of his spiritual welfare should endeavour to secure the friendship of another who fears the Lord. One way of gaining this blessing is to have no intimate friendships with those who are without God in the world. If we are known to be in close companionship with persons such as these, we shall be naturally suspected of resembling them; and good men will not come forward to seek the friendship of those who are friends of the careless and unprincipled.

Of course there are many persons whose nearest friends are already marked out for them. When men are become husbands and fathers, and still more when they are advanced in years, their nearest friendships must exist within their own households. Certainly no example is more powerful than that of him or her whose bundle of life is bound with our own. How husbands and wives can help or hinder each other in their warfare against evil! A God-fearing husband or wife influences not so much by direct exhortation as by consistent example. When Lord Peterborough had lodged for some time with Fénélon, referring to his example, he said at parting, " I shall become a Christian in spite of myself." In the same way, when one of a married pair is a sincere Christian, the other may not be able to escape becoming the same.

How miserable it is, on the other hand, when the foes to our spiritual welfare are they of our own households. This is the curse of unholy marriages, of being unequally yoked with unbelievers, and of neglecting the Christian education of our children. If such be our condition, how earnestly should we labour to hallow our earthly ties, by improving them into bonds of spiritual affection; to bring home those that are nearest and dearest to us to the knowledge of their Saviour, that as we are united to them in worldly concerns, we may not be strangers in the things which concern our everlasting peace.

XIV.

THOUGHTS FOR ADVENT.

"When a few years are come, then I shall go the way whence I shall not return."—JOB xvi. 22.

SOME people are fond of speculating about the Second Advent of our Lord. They prophesy the year and month when it is to take place. But of that day and hour knoweth no man. One thing, however, we do know, that whether the Second Coming of Christ to renew the face of the earth and to triumph over sin—whether this be sooner or later, when a few years are come we shall go to Him. There is no doubt at all about this point, and it is so important that we should often meditate upon it. We speak of the first and second Advents or Comings of Christ, but the fact is He is always coming. Are we in trouble? He comes along with the trouble and tells us to suffer as a Christian. Are success and happiness our portion? "Let Me sanctify your joy," He says, "as I did the Marriage Feast of Cana." Does strong temptation assail us? Near at hand He encourages us to fight it manfully. These are Advents or Comings of the Son of Man, who is to be our Judge as certainly as the hour of death and the great day of Assize.

We that shall die—who must die in a few months or weeks or days, but in all cases in a few years—should on certain occasions, as for instance at this Advent season, think of the absolutely certain but often forgotten fact. Though nothing in the world is more common than death, there is nothing which each one for himself finds so difficult to realize. What is death? What is the act of dying? Is it painful or not? These experiences are felt by thousands daily, for "every moment dies a man, every moment one is born," but we ourselves have never felt them; and so we half fancy that our debt to nature shall never have to be paid. How hard it is to realize that when a few more years are come each one of us shall experience death and the act of dying! Great men die, and the land mourns, and for a short time death is realized, but shall there not be one exception in our own case? Friends die, and in time we acquiesce in the inevitable, but shall a time really come in a few years when we ourselves must go over to "the majority," must leap into the "unknown dark"? Shall the day ever come when all those scenes in which we have taken part in reference to others shall be enacted in our own case? Shall we ourselves ever lie on a bed near which, it may be, will stand a table holding medicines which are prescribed not in hope of curing us, but to enable us to die more easily? There will be mysterious looks between our friends and the doctor, and then he will approach and ask us if we know our danger, and gently inform us that the last hope has fled. The few years are come, and we must go the way whence we shall not return. Nothing is more certain than that to this condition we all shall come, and yet Philip of Macedon was not more oblivious than the rest of us, though he found it necessary to order a slave to remind him every morning that he was mortal. If we would force ourselves more frequently to realize this truth, we would fear men less and God more—

> "Careless, myself a dying man,
> Of dying men's esteem;
> Happy, O Lord, if thou approve,
> Though all beside condemn."

Knowing our own weakness, littleness, and shortness of life, we must think the greatest on earth in comparison with God the mere shadow of a shade. A great French preacher expressed this feeling in a forcible way when preaching the funeral sermon over him who was called the grand monarch of France. Looking round the church, which was draped in black for the occasion, and then down on the corpse lying in state, Massillon commenced his

sermon with these words—" God alone is great ! "
Yes, He alone is great, for He changes not, while we
creatures of a day are perishing and live in the midst
of all that is perishing.

> "And then—he died. Behold before ye
> Humanity's poor sum and story ;
> Life—death—and all that is of glory."

High and low, rich and poor, one with another
await alike the inevitable hour when a few years are
come. But the thought that in a few years we shall
all be dead is certainly not one of unmixed sorrow.
To Job it was the greatest comfort. His so-called
friends told him with wearisome iteration that he
must have committed some great secret sin, or he
would not have been so greatly afflicted. The comfort of these "liars for God" was as untrue as it was
miserable, therefore it was no small relief for Job to
turn from the judgment of men to the highest Court
of Appeal—to his witness in heaven. He consoles
himself with the thought that when a few years are
come the opinion of men will not affect him in the
least. Then he shall go to Him who does not judge
according to appearances. Are we misunderstood by
friends, or full of care, anxiety and worry ? In a few
years it will all be over. Eternity be thou our refuge !
Let us do our best now, bearing and forbearing, doing
and suffering, for when "a few years are come,"
after life's fitful fever, we shall be asleep. "Death !
The unknown sea of rest ! Who knows what hidden

harmonies lie there to wrap us in softness, in eternal peace, where perhaps, and not sooner or elsewhere, all the hot longings of the soul are to be satisfied and stilled?" The time that remains is short, and in the long eternity we shall be safe, if we die in a state of grace, in the arms of Jesus. But from that way there is no return. On his death-bed a man may feel that he has wasted his life, that he has been given by God talents and opportunities which he put to no good use. He may be conscious that he has done little or no good to his fellow-creatures, but a great deal of harm. Too late now! He must go the way whence he shall not return.

Probably, the first thought of many who get to heaven will be, "Oh that I were once more upon earth to speak words of kindness to my parents, to my wife, which might atone for my unkindness. Oh that I could return to lead up to heaven those whom my example or indolence has helped down to hell. It cannot be—there is no return from that country. No return to use unused powers—no return to dry tears we have caused to flow—no return to lead to Christ those whom we have led from Him. Truly the sting of death is sin. Did we live as we ought to live, dying would be nothing worse than falling asleep. "For more than forty years," said Havelock, "I have so ruled my life that when death came I might face it without fear." Were our consciences void of offence, and had we lively faith in God's mercy through Christ and true repentance, we could say when we come to die what another great and good English general said on receiving the fatal bullet into his breast, " O death, where is thy sting ? O grave, where is thy victory ? "

" The night is far spent, the day is at hand ; let us therefore cast off the works of darkness, and put on the armour of light." The call is to awakening out of sin, carelessness, or unbelief, for the time of our going to Christ is now a year nearer to each of us. The message of Advent could hardly be better expressed than by the motto which Livingstone chose for his life—" Fear God, and work hard."

XV.

MORE THOUGHTS FOR ADVENT.

"Now the king sat in the winter-house in the ninth month: and their was a fire burning on the hearth before him. And it came to pass, that when Jehudi had read three or four leaves, he cut it with the penknife, and cast it into the fire that was on the hearth, until all the roll was consumed in the fire that was on the hearth."—JEREMIAH xxvi. 22, 23.

WE can easily picture to ourselves the scene that is brought before us. Jehoiakim, King of Judah, is sitting in his winter-house cutting a roll (the shape of book used by the ancients) with a penknife, and throwing the leaves or columns contemptuously into the brazier before which he is warming himself. What was Jehoiakim cutting and burning? It was a book in which were written God's threatenings against the sins of the king and of his people, and promises of blessing in case these sins were put away. Jehoiakim then was cutting and burning—

treating with ostentatious contempt the word of God as it was written in the Book or Bible of God.

When the prophet Jeremiah boldly rebuked the princes of Israel and Judah for their sins they, being impatient of correction and not wishing to be disturbed in their pleasant vices, shut up the prophet in prison. But the word of God that had been entrusted to Jeremiah was not to be thus silenced. Even from without the walls of his prison Jeremiah will have his message delivered. So he commands Baruch, the Scribe, to take a roll and write in it the words that he himself was unable to speak, and to read them to the princes. This Baruch does, and the princes in alarm tell the matter to the king, who sends for the roll, and orders it to be read aloud to him. But it is only a little of its contents that Jehoiakim can endure to hear. After listening for a short time he gets into an impatient rage, snatches the roll out of the hands of Baruch, cuts it with a penknife, and throws it into the fire. Several of his servants "made intercession to the king that he would not burn the roll, but he would not hear them."

If Jehoiakim, instead of burning this roll, had attended to the words written in it, he might have saved himself and his people; for the roll was really a means of grace, a hand stretched out from his heavenly Father to rescue the foolish king from impending ruin. When Jehoiakim destroyed it, he acted as foolishly as a man would do who, instead of using a fire escape put up to his window to save him from burning, would contemptuously dash it to the ground. Foolish, and even mad, we must think the act of Jehoiakim, but do we not with equal folly treat contemptuously, and refuse to avail ourselves of some of the best opportunities and most valuable means of grace? It is a sad answer most of us have to give to the question, What have I done with the gifts and blessings of God ever since I was born? He has given to me a certain amount of time, of youth, of strength, of talent, of passion, of affection, of influence — all opportunities for serving Him. What have I done with them—have I, so to speak, cut them with a penknife, and cast them into the fire?

Time is the material of our lives, but do not those people cut it with a penknife, and cast it into the fire, who talk of "killing time," and put their words into practice? But if it perishes it is recorded, and an hour will come when they would give all that they possess for a moment of it. Youth is one of the precious opportunities of life—rich in blessings if we choose to make it so, but having in it the materials of undying remorse if we cut it with a penknife, and cast it into the fire.

It is the time for settling habits, and oh! what a miserable old age is that young person laying up for himself who is settling his habits in a wrong direction. Having contemptuously abused his youth, he will understand when too late the meaning of the sad proverb which says that "the remembrance of youth is a sigh." Health is another of God's most precious gifts which is too often cut with a penknife and thrown into the fire of passionate sin. "Never treat money affairs with levity—money is character." This is a wise precept, for money is a power lent to us by God, not for our own use only, but for the good of others. There is then such a thing as conscientious money-spending, and it is very sinful to cut money, so to speak, with a penknife and cast it into the fire.

Let us remember that if we do in this way cut with a penknife and contemptuously waste God's best gifts, let us remember that a day will come when He will say to us, "Give an account of thy stewardship, for thou mayest be no longer steward. I gave thee a life which might have been a blessing to thy fellow-men—why have its powers been guiltily neglected, or guiltily squandered? I gave thee a body full of strength and health—how is it enfeebled by folly and excess? I gave thee a mind capable of making thee wise and noble—why is it like a sluggard's garden, full of thorns? I gave thee the power of loving, influencing, and sympathizing with others, and hast thou dared to cut these opportunities with a penknife and to cast them into the fire?"

If we are to be saved, we must use the means of salvation which God gives to us as He gave this roll of a book to Jehoiakim. Above all, we must not treat with contempt the gracious invitations of our Saviour to come unto Him. If we despise or neglect so great salvation, we shall kill our souls. The soul of man is like a curious chamber with elastic walls, which can be expanded with God as its guest almost to infinity, but which without God shrinks and shrivels until every vestige of the Divine is gone. One cannot call what is left a soul; it is a shrunken, useless organ, a capacity sentenced to death by disuse, which droops as a withered hand by the side, and cumbers nature like a rotten branch.

No doubt Jehoiakim fancied when he burned the roll upon which God's threatenings against his sins were written, that these would somehow be prevented from taking effect. But the truth of God is not so easily destroyed. Jeremiah caused another and a longer roll to be written. "Then took Jeremiah another roll, and gave it to Baruch the Scribe, the son of Neriah; who wrote therein from the mouth of Jeremiah all the words of the book which Jehoiakim, King of Judah, had burned in the fire: and there were added besides unto them many like words."

From this we may learn the often forgotten fact that the truth of God does not depend upon men. They may believe or they may not believe, but though this matters to themselves it cannot destroy truth. If the whole world ceased to believe in Christianity, not one jot or tittle of its truth would perish—

> "Truth wounded yet shall live again,
> The immortal years of God are hers;
> But error wounded writhes in pain,
> And dies amidst her worshippers."

It is well to remember this fact, which, when stated, seems so obvious, for many men have a contemptuous, patronizing way of talking about religion as if it would perish if they ceased to believe it. When they hear of some great man or of a large number of men becoming unbelievers, they fancy that there is safety for their own unbelief in numbers, and that the mere prevalency of unbelief can destroy eternal truth.

And as it is with truth, so is it with our responsibilities. We do not get rid of them by simply ignoring them and treating them with contempt. Many thus act as regards those seasons which have been appointed by the Church to be opportunities for instruction and spiritual culture, quite forgetting that they shall be held responsible for the way they use them. These are times of refreshing if rightly used; but if we cut them with a penknife and cast them away, how shall we escape greater condemnation? May we not be guilty of doing so with Advent, which comes once more to fix our thoughts on man's sin and its awful responsibility!

The season of Advent, with which the Church opens her year, proclaims the approach of our Lord Jesus Christ. The name (which signifies coming) speaks to us of the two comings of our blessed Saviour—the first, in mercy to save; the second, in terror to judge. The terrors of the Lord are brought before us in the epistle for Advent Sunday, rousing us as it does from our sleep of sin and sloth. "The night is far spent, the day is at hand." In Helen's tower, which is built half-way up Belfast Lough, there is a bed with this inscription—

> "I nightly pitch my moving tent
> A day's march nearer home."

It is well to think this every night when we lay our heads on the pillow. Each evening finds us one day nearer to our last day than the preceding one left us, but each Advent brings us one year closer either to the coming of our Saviour to us or of our going to Him. "Our salvation is nearer than when we believed."

No wonder then that the first lesson for Advent Sunday opens with a loud call to repentance. The heavens and the earth are aroused to listen and give ear while the Lord pleads with His people, setting before them their sins and His mercies. But it is the same with all parts of all the services of this solemn season. They tell us how He who once came to dwell visibly amongst His people now dwells invisibly, though not less surely, among them by His Holy Word and sacraments; that by His "still small voice" speaking to us in them, He might prepare us for the day when the sound of His voice shall no longer gently invite, but shall shake earth and heaven in calling us to judgment. Shall we cut with a penknife and treat with contempt these terrible warnings and gracious invitations?

XVI.

CHRISTMAS THOUGHTS.

"There was no room in the inn."—LUKE ii. 7.

AFTER the creation of the world, the birth of Christ is the most important event in history. To every single human being Christmas Day ought to be the greatest day in the year. Why? Because, when Christ was born, the mighty God revealed to His creatures who were feeling after and ignorantly worshipping Him, that His highest nature is loving and full of tender mercy. Christ's own words, "He that hath seen Me hath seen the Father also," teach us that His incarnation has enabled us to know the invisible and infinite God, as we need to know Him, and as mankind has always craved to know Him.

On Christmas Day we assert our belief in the Divinity of Christ in such phrases as—"There was always something in the inconceivable and infinite God which had sympathy for and affinity with human nature. There was, so to speak, a human side in God. What could be so expressed—the human side, the moral and affectional attributes—these came forth in Jesus Christ; He revealed them." He was God-Man as representing God to man, and He was Man-God as presenting man before God. We are then celebrating the birth of a real Saviour, the Friend of humanity.

"The Man of Sorrows," the Man also of "joy unspeakable, and full of glory," and "The Author and Finisher of our Faith."

The incarnation of our Saviour reveals what has been called "The Good Shepherd side of God." It tells us that the Divine heart is touched with the feeling of our infirmities. God's highest nature was shown to us when Jesus said—"Come unto Me, all ye that labour and are heavy laden;" when He wept over the grave of friendship and the city of Jerusalem; when He sanctified all the business, innocent joys, and sorrows of life, and proved to us that nothing human is indifferent to Him.

> "He took the suffering human race,
>   He read each wound, each weakness clear,
>   He struck His finger on the place
>   And said, 'Thou ailest here and here.'"

But the Great Physician did not merely find out our ailments and sympathize with them in words. "He went on to help in time of need." In His life He went about doing good, and He died to prove that God loves us sinners as much as He hates our sin. In this way, then, we believe that the eternally human side of God became incarnate, came forth and dwelt amongst us as it has never before or since; that then and there, in the fulness of time, amongst the chosen people, and in the Holy Land, 1900 years ago, a special use of human nature was made for a special purpose, and we "beheld His glory, the glory as of the only-begotten of the Father, full of grace and truth." It is true we cannot in the least understand the incarnation, but if we are to limit our creed by our understanding, it will be limited indeed. We cannot understand the nature of God nor even the nature of man, so it is no wonder that the union of the two in Christ should be the "mystery of mysteries."

Again, the greatness of the condescension, while it ought to fill us with gratitude, is sometimes almost more than we can believe. God is so great and we are so little, can it be that His only-begotten Son visited us and tabernacled in our flesh? Is not the message of Christmas too good news to be true?

In the eighth Psalm, David represents himself gazing up into the heavens, and being filled with wonder at the glory of God as seen in the star-lit sky. Then the thought came into his mind—how small and insignificant is man in comparison with these worlds rising upon worlds; can it be that the great Creator is mindful of him: does He indeed visit him, or is he not greatly below His notice?

"When I consider Thy heavens, the work of Thy fingers, the moon and the stars, which Thou hast ordained; what is man that Thou art mindful of him? and the son of man that Thou visitest him?" Now certainly if man seemed an insignificant being when weighed against David's scanty knowledge of the number and magnitude of the stars, it is only natural for us to fall sometimes into a similar train of melancholy thought, when we read the sublime accounts which astronomers now give us of these same stars. Had David known, what every schoolboy now knows, that there are twenty millions of stars within the range of the telescope, and out of range millions more in infinite space, and that there is no reason for supposing even these to exhaust the limits of creation—had he known this, with how much greater meaning would he have asked this question—"What is man that Thou art mindful of him, or the son of man that Thou visitest him?"

But if David's difficulty was less than ours, because he knew less of the stars, and imagined our little earth to be the centre of creation, we have a consoling answer to his question, of which he was ignorant, for we see Jesus, who is not ashamed to call us "brethren." Man may be almost nothing in comparison with the forces of the universe; but still God *has* visited him.

"The Word was made flesh, and dwelt amongst

us." The incarnation enables us to lift up our heads in the face of the overwhelming spaces, masses, and forces which surround us, and to believe that a human being, having a knowledge of his own existence, and knowing good and evil, is more valuable in God's sight than any amount of unconscious, lifeless matter. The fact that our Lord Jesus Christ has taken upon Himself man's nature, is a truth which, if really believed, would for ever dispel all unworthy doubts concerning the dignity and destiny of man, and God's fatherly care for the whole human race. "Forasmuch as the children are partakers of flesh and blood, He also Himself likewise took part in the same." All cynical contempt for mankind is done away by this fact. All despair of nations is at once destroyed; all notions of superiority over our brother man; all hopelessness as to the final triumph of good over evil, blessedness over misery. From whatever antecedents man has either fallen or risen, he was somehow capable of imparting to the Son of God his nature, and of being perfected by suffering, by blessings, by all means, into the glorious image of God, his Redeemer. In the words of Isaiah, we may say that the incarnation of Christ has made " a man more precious than fine gold ; even a man than the gold wedge of Ophir."

With a wonderful condescension, Christ came emptying Himself of the glory which He had with the Father before the world was. He became the Son of Man; mortal, but not a sinner; heir of our infirmities, not of our guiltiness ; the offspring of the old race, yet the beginning of the new "creation of God." He came into this world, not in the clouds of heaven, but born into it—born of a woman. And when He had reached man's estate, He began His ministry, preached the gospel, went about doing good, suffered on the cross, died, and was buried, rose again and ascended on high, there to reign till the day when He comes again to judge the world. This is the all-gracious mystery of the incarnation, which we do well, at this season, to look into and adore. Throughout the world there was more or less of preparation for the birth of Christ. The Jewish prophets foretold it. The completion of the Roman Empire, which facilitated the spread of the gospel, was accomplished. Even heathen writers inform us that at the time there was a vague but very general expectation that some wonderful event was at hand. The ancient religions had lost their savour, and society was falling into moral decay.

Thus it was that Christ came in the fulness of time, and was the desire of all nations.

But though there was preparation in the world at large, little of it was made for the Saviour's birth in Bethlehem. The circumstances of that birth are related in the second lesson for Christmas Morning Service. The people go up to Jerusalem to be enrolled for taxation purposes. For mutual convenience they form themselves into caravans. The sudden influx of strangers completely filled one of the inns on the way, and Mary and Joseph were obliged to take the only accommodation available—that of a stable. Thus it was that Jesus was born in lowliness and want, amid the tumults of a mixed multitude; cast aside into the outhouse of a crowded inn; laid to His first rest among brute cattle. There was no place for Christ in the inn. Can this be said of the inn of our hearts? If so, though the season of Christmas may bring to us feasting and excitement, we have no real happiness. Our joy is selfish and unconsecrated. We cannot go into the loneliness of our chamber and think. The burden of sin weighs us down, and we are still in bondage to the fear of death. We are all wishing our friends a happy Christmas and New Year; but the wish is vain if there be no room for Christ in the inn.

On the other hand, how full of happiness would this season be to any one who, by meditating on its holy mysteries, could feel that Christ was being more and more clearly seen of him as of one born out of due time! So may we hope that the fulness of the blessings brought to us on Christmas Day may shed itself over our whole lives; that, having received "power to become the sons of God," through the mercy of Him who became Son of Man, we may daily be renewed in His image, until we come to the "measure of the stature of the fulness of Christ." There was no room for Him in the inn at Bethlehem, but by His help we will take care that neither business, nor pleasure, nor sin crowd Him out of our hearts.

"Wrapped in His swaddling bands,
  And in His manger laid,
The Hope and Glory of all lands
  Is come to the world's aid:
No peaceful home upon His cradle smiled,
Guests rudely went and came where slept the royal child.

But where Thou dwellest, Lord,
  No other thought should be,
Once duly welcomed and adored,
  How shall I part with Thee?
Bethlehem must lose Thee soon, but Thou wilt grace
The single heart to be Thy sure abiding-place."

XVII.

THE DIVINE ARITHMETIC OF LIFE.

"So teach us to number our days, that we may apply our hearts unto wisdom."—PSALM xc. 12.

THE sojourn of the Israelites in the wilderness had been prolonged to forty years, in order that the whole generation which had come out of Egypt might die. It would seem to have been towards the end of that time when the aged people of the congregation were continually dropping off at seventy or eighty years of age that this psalm, entitled "A prayer of Moses the man of God," was written. No wonder then that in it every image suggestive of uncertainty and transitoriness should be used to describe human life. It is compared to the swiftly passing shuttle of the weaver, to a watch in the night from which the watcher is soon relieved, to the rushing past of a water-flood, to a leaf green in the morning, dried up and withered in the evening.

These are not artificial images, but natural. They were not used by Moses because of their prettiness, but were forced upon him by their truthfulness and by the circumstances of the pilgrimage in the wilderness.

If ever we ought to practise what has been called the Divine arithmetic of life, it is at the close of one year and the beginning of another. In garrison towns there is a cannon fired at noon, and when people not accustomed to it hear it for the first time, they generally start and say "Oh my!" so that the gun is often called by soldiers the "Oh my!" People are startled by the noise, but they might start too at the thought of how quickly each day passes. How much more ought we to feel the passing of a year, and how quickly has 1886 become 1887!

Time is a river that never ceases to flow, and each New Year's Day must make even the most thoughtless realize in some degree that their own little streamlet is gliding away, and bearing them along with it towards that awful other world of which all things here are but the shadows. "When Wilkie was in the Escurial," says Southey, "looking at Titian's famous picture of the Last Supper in the refectory there, an old Jeronymite monk said to him, 'I have sat daily in sight of that picture for now nearly threescore years; during that time my companions have dropped off one after another—all who were my seniors, all who were my contemporaries, and many or most of those who were younger than myself; more than one generation has passed away, and there the figures in the picture have remained unchanged. I look at them, till I sometimes think that *they* are the realities, and *we* are but shadows.'"

What this picture did for the monk, New Year's Day should do for all of us—force upon us the thought that our days on the earth are as a shadow, and that there is none abiding.

"What is your life?" This question was asked by St. James of certain persons who seemed never to have meditated upon the changes and chances of this mortal life. The apostle missed in these people one of the surest marks of Christian earnestness. The uncertainty of human life had not become a fixed image in their minds—"Go to now, ye that say, To-day or to-morrow we will go into such a city, and continue there a year, and buy and sell, and get gain: whereas ye know not what shall be on the morrow. For what is your life? It is even a vapour, that appeareth for a little time, and then vanisheth away. It saddened the soul of St. James to see men believing that they could insure the future—forming all sorts of plans in utter forgetfulness of the fact that "Man proposes, God disposes." The following incident is related in the life of Dr. Arnold. "There had never," writes his biographer, " been a time from his earliest manhood in which the uncertainty of human life had not been one of the fixed images in his mind; and many instances would recur to all who knew him of the way in which it was constantly blended with all his thoughts of the future. 'Shall I tell you, my little boy,' he once said to one of his younger children, whose joyful glee at the approaching holidays he had gently rebuked, 'shall I tell you why I call it sad?' He then repeated to him the simple story of his own early childhood: how his own father had made him read to him a sermon on the text, 'Boast not thyself of to-morrow,' on the Sunday evening before his sudden death. 'Now cannot you see, when you talk with such certainty about this day week and what we shall do, why it seems sad to me?'"

A few years of thoughtless boyhood; the dream of early youth, from which we soon awake to the realities of middle life; and then, after possibly a short time of waiting, we are gone. It is a tale soon told. No wonder that St. James thus answers his own question, What is your life? "It is even a vapour that appeareth for a little time, and then vanisheth away." Sometimes this truth is impressed upon us when we see a crowd of thousands of people, and reflect that in fifty years scarcely any of them will be alive.

They are now speaking of giving fixity of tenure in land; but what no man can give either to himself or to any one else is fixity of tenure in life. We are all tenants, liable to be ejected without an hour's notice. "It fareth," says an old writer, "with most men's lives as with the sand in a deceptive hour-glass; look but upon it in outward appearance, and it seemeth far more than it is, because it riseth up upon the sides, whilst the sand is empty and hollow in the midst thereof; so that when it sinks down in an instant, a quarter of an hour is gone in a moment. Thus many men are mistaken in their own account, reckoning upon threescore and ten years as the age of a man, because their bodies seem strong and lusty. Alas! their health may be hollow, there may be some inward infirmity and imperfection unknown to them, so that death may surprise them on a sudden, and they be cut down like the grass."

There are a thousand gates to death, through one of which we may have to pass before the end of another year. The Emperor Justinian died by going into a room which had been newly painted; Pope Adrian was strangled by a fly; a consul struck his foot against his own threshold, and his foot mortified, so that he died thereby. Men have been choked by a grape stone, killed by a tile falling from the roof of a house, poisoned by a drop, carried off by a whiff of foul air. St. Augustine might well say that he did not know whether to call our life a dying life or a living death. We are always dying. In the morning we cannot make sure of the evening, nor in the evening can we reckon upon the morning. How much less can we be sure of seeing the end of a new year. "Lord, make me to know mine end, and the measure of my days, what it is; let me know how frail I am."

But, it may be asked, what is the use of dwelling on such sad reflections? Why should we number our days? The writer of this ninetieth Psalm gives a very good reason for so doing. "So teach us," he says, "to number our days that we may apply our hearts unto wisdom.'" Certainly the days may be numbered, and the heart *not* applied to wisdom. Those who say, "Let us eat and drink: for tomorrow we die," number their days that they may apply their hearts unto *folly*. There is a strong tendency to do this when the time is felt to be short and religion does not exist.

Nor is it any part of Christian duty to think of the shortness of life in an abject spirit. "That which the demoniac in the Gospels did, having his dwelling among the tombs, has sometimes been reckoned the perfection of Christian unworldliness. Men have looked on every joy as a temptation; on every earnest pursuit as a snare—the skull and the hour-glass their companions, covering life with melancholy, haunting it with visions and emblems of mortality." This is not Christianity. Rather it is so to dwell on thoughts of death "that we may apply our hearts unto wisdom." Instead of paralyzing action, this sort of meditation urges us to make the most of our lives. He is the best prepared to meet change who sees it at a distance and contemplates it calmly. Affections are never deepened and refined until the possibility of loss is felt. Duty is done with energy in proportion as we realize that "The night cometh when no man can work."

Most of us must feel remorse as we look back on the year that has gone so quickly from us. An epitome of its history might, it is to be feared, be written for many in the words of Daniel—"O Lord, to us belongeth confusion of face, because we have sinned against Thee." We have known fond mothers who got their children photographed annually to compare the pictures and see the progress that had been made. Were our spiritual photographs compared with those of last year, would we be found to have grown in grace? Have we been as happy as we might have been; have we done any acts of purely unselfish kindness; has any one been much the better for our existence during the past year; have we offered up one uninterrupted prayer? Let the walls of our chambers speak; let our churches, houses, offices speak. Are we more trusting in God and more useful to man?

If we think back and honestly ask ourselves a few searching questions like these, last year can scarcely fail to make us self-reproachful. But the year is gone beyond recall, and about it we can only ask—

> "Whose hands shall dare to open and explore
> Those volumes, closed and clasped for evermore?
> Not mine. With reverential feet I pass,
> I hear a voice that cries, 'Alas! alas!
> Whatever hath been written shall remain,
> Nor be erased, nor written o'er again;
> The unwritten only belongs to thee,
> Take heed and ponder well what that shall be.'"

To us belongeth confusion of face, for neither as

individuals nor as a nation have we during the past year obeyed the voice of the Lord our God. The heart sickens at the thought of past sinfulness. Every closing year seems to say, Shall we begin the old struggle over again? Yes, for to the Lord our God belong mercies and forgivenesses. If we are sorry and tell Him so, He will not be extreme to mark what is done amiss in the old year and will help us to do better in the new. As the tree is fertilized by its own broken branches and fallen leaves, so may our souls grow out of broken hopes and disappointing failures. We enter upon a new year praying God to give us beauty for ashes, and to prosper the work of our hands for Jesus Christ's sake.

XVIII.

EXCUSES.

"And the man said, The woman whom Thou gavest to be with me, she gave me of the tree, and I did eat. And the Lord God said unto the woman, What is this that thou hast done? And the woman said, The serpent beguiled me, and I did eat."
—Genesis iii. 12, 13.

IN their childhood nations are very imaginative. They are fond of allegories and parables, and the sacred books of all ancient religions make these the vehicles for conveying deep spiritual truths. In such cases we must separate the form of the story from the truth it contains. Whatever men think about the details of the fall of Adam and Eve, they cannot deny that it is the allegory of a moral fact—man's highest nature conquered by his lower feelings.

Do not our first parents appear to start forth into life from the pages of this old Book as we read the two verses which relate the excuses they made for their disobedience? They seem no longer merely characters in a history, but flesh-and-blood breathing realities, for, perhaps, it was only yesterday, or even to-day, that we tried to deceive our consciences with excuses quite as weak and not very unlike these: "The woman whom Thou gavest to be with me, she gave me of the tree, and I did eat." "The serpent beguiled me, and I did eat."

"Say not thou," says the Son of Sirach, "It is through the Lord that I fell away; for thou oughtest not to do the things that He hateth. Say not thou, He hath caused me to err." This is just what Adam and Eve did say. When accused of disobedience they retorted, and dared to blame God for their sin. "If only thou hadst given me a wife proof against temptation," says Adam. "If only the serpent had never been created," says Eve.

Very similar are most of the excuses we make. We blame the gifts that God gives us rather than ourselves, and turn that free will which would make us only a little lower than the angels if rightly used, into a "heritage of woe." A man has a bad temper, is careless about his home, and is led to eat the forbidden fruit of unlawful pleasures. When his conscience asks him, "Hast thou eaten of the tree, whereof I commanded thee that thou shouldest not eat?" He answers, "It's all my wife's fault. She provokes my temper by her extravagance, carelessness, and fondness for staying away from home. She does not make my home home-like, so I am driven to solace myself with unlawful pleasures." "The woman whom Thou gavest to be with me, she gave me of the tree, and I did eat."

And wives are not less ready to make the conduct of husbands an excuse for a low tone of thought and religion. They ask how it is possible for them to retain their youthful desire of serving Christ when their husbands make home wretched and sneer at everything high and holy. "Easy it is for others to be good, but for myself I find that a wife cannot be better than her husband will allow her to be."

How often is ill-health pleaded as an excuse for bad temper and selfishness! If we are rich, we allow ourselves to be idle and luxurious. If poor, we think that while it is easy to be good on ten thousand a year, it is impossible for us to resist the temptations of poverty. Is a man without self-restraint and self-control? He thinks it enough to say that his passions are very strong. In the time of joy and prosperity we are careless and thoughtless. When sorrow comes to us, we become hard and unbelieving, and we think that the joy and the sorrow should quite excuse us.

Again, evil-doers say that no man could do otherwise were he in their position, that there is no living at their trade honestly, that their health requires this and that indulgence, that nobody could be religious in the house in which they live, and so on. If God wanted us to fight the good fight of faith in other places and under other circumstances, He would move us, but He wishes us to begin the battle where we are, and not elsewhere. There subdue everything that stands in conflict with the law of conscience, and the law of love, and the law of purity, and the law of truth. Begin the fight wherever God sounds the trumpet, and He will give you grace, that as your day is, so your strength shall be. As long as people say, " I cannot help it," they will not help it; but if they will only try their best they will be able to say, " I can do all things through Christ who strengtheneth me."

On comparing the excuses which we modern sinners make with those attributed in the text to the first sinners, Adam and Eve, we find one circumstance characterizing them both. We, as well as they, virtually say, that only for difficulty and temptation, we would be very good. And yet how absurd it would be to give a Victoria Cross for bravery in the *absence* of the enemy. We would all laugh if we heard a man greatly praised for being honest and sober when in prison, because we would know that it was impossible for him to be anything else. It is just because the Christian life is not an easy thing, that at our baptism we are signed with the sign of the Cross, in token that we shall have to fight manfully under His banner against sin, the world, and the devil. Do we complain that this manful fight is a necessity? It would not be possible for us to be good without it. If we had not the power of going wrong, we could deserve no reward for going right. Why, then, should we make the possibility of virtue an excuse for vice?

"Often excusing of a fault doth make the fault the worse by the excuse," for it adds lying and moral cowardice to it. It requires considerable courage to say simply as David did, without blaming any person or anything or making the slightest excuse, "I have sinned against the Lord."

But, indeed, the man who keeps his eyes upon God, and not upon his neighbour, is little prone to deceive himself with untrue excuses. When we have only a hearsay knowledge of God, we are satisfied with ourselves and think it quite enough to be no worse than the multitude of men who do evil. Not so, however, when we see God ourselves. Then we say with Job, "I had heard of thee by the hearing of the ear; but now mine eye seeth thee, *wherefore* I abhor myself, and repent in dust and ashes." Some of us may not feel as we ought, sorrow for our sins, and the reason may be because we have only heard of God with the hearing of the ear, and have never seen Him ourselves.

A very small occurrence may give us that sight-knowledge of God which makes us know ourselves. A man walking along a street was given a tract by some one whom he considered troublesome, but who meant well. He tore it, and flung the pieces to the winds. Another man passing along afterwards saw one of the pieces. It only contained one word, but it was one that made him think. That word was "Eternity." It made him think of the shortness of man's life, and that soon he would be called upon to give an account of his thoughts, words, and deeds. At that moment he saw God, and saw himself, and repented of his want of service.

There was an excuse for Job hearing of God only by the hearing of the ear, but we can see Jesus who is the express image for us of God. Therefore, we are not to compare ourselves with our neighbours, but with the Perfect Man, Jesus Christ.

Away then with all excuses! In the spirit of the Publican and not in that of the Pharisee, let us approach Almighty God. Without one plea or the smallest excuse we may go to our Saviour. If passion rises in thee, go to Him as a demoniac. If deadness creeps upon thee, go in the spirit of the paralytic. If darkness clouds thy face, go as Bartimæus. And when thou prayest, go always as a leper crying as Isaiah did, " Unclean! Unclean! " Let us do this, and then we shall feel the meaning of those words which are so often spoken, but so little felt: " If we say that we have no sin, we deceive ourselves, and the truth is not in us; but if we confess our sins, He is faithful and just to forgive us our sins, and to cleanse us from all unrighteousness."

XIX.

SECRET FAULTS.

"Who can understand his errors? cleanse thou me from secret faults."—Psalm xix. 12.

JESUS CHRIST when on earth was sneered at and despised by persons who considered themselves highly respectable, and on the whole very good sort of people. It is so now. As long as we are careless and well pleased with ourselves, so long must His message of loving forgiveness appear "foolishness" unto us. We cannot greatly desire to have the burden of sin taken from us if we never have felt it at all. It is only when we are forced to cry out "to us belongeth confusion of face," that we are induced to throw ourselves upon what follows: "To the Lord our God belong mercies and forgivenesses." Confession must go before absolution— David had to say unto Nathan, "I have sinned against the Lord," before Nathan could assure him that the Lord had put away his sin. The first thing to be done in order to appreciate the message of forgiveness of sin, is to try and understand our errors.

Let us, then, at this solemn season of Lent, resolutely determine to undergo the pain of knowing ourselves in order that the shame which we shall feel, if our self-examination be at all honestly done, may force us to ask for mercy at the throne of Grace —Cleanse Thou me, O God, from secret faults, for the sake of Thy dear Son who came not to call the righteous but sinners to repentance!

But it may be asked, Do we not all understand our errors? Do we not call ourselves " miserable offenders" in the Confession, and "miserable sinners" in the Litany? Yes, but such general acknowledgment of sin is very far removed from knowledge and hatred of our particular errors and secret faults. We too often mean no more when we say that we are miserable sinners than this—that as no man is perfectly good, so we are tainted with human imperfection. Now certainly it does not require much humility to confess that we are offenders, if we mean no more by the acknowledgment than what might be said of St. John, of St. Paul, and of all God's best servants in every age. It is easy to say vaguely, " I am a miserable sinner;" it is not quite so easy to say, "Last Monday I told this or that lie, on Tuesday I was guilty of a certain mean action, and neglected my duty on this or that occasion," and so on.

Those who feel most free from secret faults are just those who have most of them. The best men are the most humble and the most charitable towards the failings of others; for having a higher standard of excellence in their minds than others have, and knowing themselves better, they see the breadth and depth of their own sinful nature, and are shocked and frightened at themselves.

It is no easy matter to understand our errors, and to know ourselves even as other men know us, much less as God does. If we would discover how many faults we have of which we ourselves are ignorant, we should reflect that we can clearly see the failings of others of which they know nothing. As, then, we can see the sins of others, so we ourselves must have many faults which are secret to us now, but of which we would become aware if some power would give us the gift of seeing ourselves as others see us. Another way in which we may come to a knowledge of our real character is to keep a steady eye on the suspicious part of it. Suppose, then, a man fully satisfied with himself, one who thinks he is a very respectable, truly Christian person, one who considers that he is "saved" without clearly understanding from what he is saved. Well, granting this opinion you have of yourself to be a correct one, yet as every one is liable to be mistaken, consider what part of your character would an enemy first fix on if he wished to abuse you, and what faults would your neighbours be most ready to believe that you had.

Look, then, to this part of your character, and you may find that all is not as well there as you now fancy it is.

One cannot but be touched by that story which some wise sanitary observer made known to the public. He noticed how a young woman who had come up to London from the country, and was living in some miserable court or alley, made for a time great efforts to keep that court or alley clean. But gradually, day by day, the efforts of the poor woman were less and less vigorous, until in a few weeks she became accustomed to, and contented with, the state of filth which surrounded her, and made no further efforts to remove it. The atmosphere she lived in was too strong for her.

The same difficulty is felt in resisting our errors and secret faults, but not to resist is fatal. A man is tempted to lie, to steal, to wrong his neighbour, to indulge some bad passion, and resolves to do it only once, and thinks that "just once" cannot matter. Oh, pause! That one sin is the trickling rill which becomes the bounding torrent, the broad river, the waste, troubled, discoloured sea. You drop a stone out of your hand: it is the law of gravitation that, if it falls twelve feet the first second, it will fall forty-eight feet the next second, and 108 feet the third second, and 300 feet the fifth second; and that, if it falls for ten seconds, in the last second it will rush through 1,200 feet of air. Even with that rapidly increasing momentum, even with that rushing swiftness, is the increase and multiplication of unchecked sin falling on and on, until it is dashed to shivers on the rock of death.

Frequently during Lent we should ask ourselves what are the bad habits that are beginning to be formed in us? We should take the different spheres of life, and examine our conduct as regards each of them. Let us judge ourselves that we be not judged of the Lord in reference to our business, our home, our pleasures. What sort of books do we read? Do we think before we speak, or are we in the habit of saying things in society which any one present might reasonably wish to be unsaid? Are we guilty of secret sins in thought or deed? Do we pray as we ought? Does our charity suffer long and is it kind, or are we impatient and overbearing towards others? How have we been getting on since last Lent, not in pocket but in character? Are we more manly or more womanly, more true, more humble, more loving? Our duty to God and our neighbour is so and so, how have we done it? Above all, do we think of Christ as our King and personal Saviour, or is all we really know of Him the sound of His name and the words about Him in the Creeds? These are questions which it is painful for me to ask just because they are suggested by my own shortcomings. It would be much more pleasant to talk of subtle points of doctrine unconnected with practical every-day life, and to cheat myself and you with soft pretty phrases, as though Christianity were not intended to make us better men and women.

Do any now ask, "Why should I trouble about my errors, why should I seek to be cleansed from my secret faults? There may be another world, and what preachers say may be true, but as I am no worse than thousands of others, why should I not let well enough alone?" I know that many have such thoughts, for they often occur to myself, so it may not be useless to briefly suggest three strong reasons why we should endeavour to lay aside the sin that doth so easily beset us. The first thought is, that we have not to fight the battle alone. If we believe our Saviour's words, "Lo, I am with you alway, even unto the end," we believe that in all our struggles against evil, as in all our troubles, we have a very present Help. Gerizim and Ebal, blessing and cursing, good and evil, light and darkness, life and death, may be struggling for the possession of our souls; but if our heart be right with God, if we are humble and faithful, if we watch and pray, we are safe now, and shall be for ever. Christ is neither dead nor absent. "Alas, my master! how shall we do? And he answered, Fear not: for they that be with us are more than they that be with them."

The next reason why we should struggle after self-improvement is because "whatsoever a man soweth that shall he also reap." In our business, in our recreations, in everything we do, we are influencing our future destiny. The child is father to the man, and the man goes to his own place. What we are is what we have been, and what we shall be is what we are.

A light-hearted lad passes through a wood, and thoughtlessly strikes a young oak sapling. The scar heals over, but when that tree is cut down a thousand years afterwards that blow is written on its heart. As heedlessly he puts the first thought of impurity into the soul of another, innocent up to that moment, and, owing to that thought perhaps, that soul is lost.

The third reason is because nothing worldly lasts. Too many of us busy ourselves about everything except the Kingdom of God and its righteousness, but silently, surely day follows upon day, year upon year, youth upon childhood, old age upon youth, until that hour comes when, even from the most worldly, the world passeth away and the lust thereof.

> "Then, O my Lord, prepare
> My soul for that great day;
> O wash me in Thy precious blood,
> And take my sins away."

XX.

"*IS IT NOT A LITTLE ONE?*"

> "I cannot escape to the mountain, lest evil overtake me, and I die: behold now, this city is near to flee unto, and it is a little one: Oh, let me escape thither (is it not a little one?) and my soul shall live."—GENESIS xix. 20.

IN these pleading words Lot answered the angels who told him to escape for his life from the doomed cities of the plain. He shrinks from breaking up the habits and associations of his life. The moral atmosphere of the mountain where he is ordered to go may be much purer, but a certain amount of danger, difficulty, and hardship will have to be encountered there. Could not one city be saved to afford him a refuge? We should expect that after all the marvellous mercy shown by God to Lot, he would have been ready to go wherever commanded. But no; he asks that Zoar may be saved. "Behold now, this city is near to flee unto, and it is a little one : Oh, let me escape thither (is it not a little one ?) "

Brethren, may not a spiritual application be given to this story, one that touches ourselves and is very suitable for consideration at the season of Lent ? God warns us to flee from the low-level life of sin to the mountain of purity and peace. A word spoken by a friend, something read in a letter or book, joy, sorrow, anything God can use as His angel or messenger to call us away from the land of sin. He invites us to be sorry for the past, to turn to Him, to put away the evil of our doings, to give Him our hearts. And we are willing to do so on condition that we may keep that one little sin that doth so easily beset us. There is one habit which conscience tells us is not quite right, but which could only be broken by a painful struggle. It is not a crime or a great sin, and some people speak lightly of it and hardly think it a sin at all. If it be a sin, it certainly is not a great one. Oh, let me keep this sin (is it not a little one ?), and all other sins I shall put away.

But this sort of compromise is impossible. The contagion of any one conscious sin, however small, will poison the whole soul. God will have all of a man's heart, or none of it. " One thing thou lackest," He says, if we keep a Zoar, though we may give up all other things. The distinction we draw between little and great sins is probably a survival of the old scholastic division between " venial" and " deadly sins," but this distinction is altogether delusive, for all sins are venial if repented of, and no sin is venial, or, as we say, a little one, if it be indulged long enough to harden the heart and to make it incapable of repentance. The little city of Zoar was spared at Lot's request, but here the parallel ceases, for God will not allow us to keep even one little conscious sin, or if He does, it is only in order that it may become its own punishment.

It is well to judge ourselves that we be not judged of the Lord, and we could not do better than try and discover this Lent what the little Zoar is in which we have taken refuge. What is that one sin to which we fondly cling when others are being put away? Probably it is not what is called a great sin in the eyes of men. Our temptation is to the commission of sins which the world considers quite respectable. Indeed it may be taken for granted that all here are free from flagrant crimes and great conscious sins, for great criminals and notorious sinners seldom attend special week-day services in church. The mere fact of your presence proves that on the whole and in great matters you desire to serve God; but when great sins were put away, was there no little Zoar retained? Your conscience told you that whatever the Zoar was it should go with the rest; but you pleaded for it in the very words of Lot—" Is it not a little one?"

Let us think of some of the reasons why we should try by God's grace to put away those little sins which we have been comparing to the little Zoar for which Lot pleaded. The first reason is because in God's sight there is no such thing as a little sin. He is of purer eyes than to behold with tolerance any evil. Men speak of a sin as being little, because they cannot see its far-reaching consequences and all the harm it does; but to the omniscient God, what is called a little sin may appear a very great one.

Then we ought to reflect that doing conspicuous good actions and abstaining from great sins cannot prove our love to God as much as doing small duties and abstaining from little sins. Without caring in the smallest degree for goodness, we may avoid crime and gross sin because of the police, or because we desire to get on in the world, or because we are afraid of what people say. The test, therefore, of a fine character is attention to what are called the small matters of conduct.

We are to take up our cross *daily*. This expression proves that the course of self-denial which Christ prescribes consists in little things, for great efforts would not be required every day.

Another reason why we should be afraid to harbour little sins is because they lead to great ones. It has been remarked that we cannot change even a particle of sand on the sea-shore to a different place without changing at the same time the balance of the globe. The earth's centre of gravity will be altered by the action, in an infinitely small degree no doubt, but still altered; and upon this will ensue climatic change which may influence people's temperaments and actions. Of course this is an absurd refinement, but it illustrates the undoubted fact that the most trivial thought and act in our lives carries with it a train of consequences, the end of which we may never guess. We are not worst at once; the course of evil begins from a slight source, but

> " Small habits well pursued betimes
> May reach the dignity of crimes."

"I've seen pretty clearly," says Adam Bede in George Eliot's story, "ever since I could cast up a sum, that you can never do what is wrong without breeding sin and trouble, more than you can ever see. It's like a bit of bad workmanship; you never see the end of the mischief it will do." The convict did not think that he would ever steal when he took the loan of some money out of his master's till, intending to put it back in a day or two. The drunkard may have boasted that he never would exceed the bounds of strict moderation, but he gradually grew fond of alcohol, at first in moderate drinking—day by day a little increased, year by year a little multiplied by the solitary becoming the frequent, and the frequent the habitual, and the habitual the all-but-inevitable transgression. You are not actually bad—indeed you may be in a measure good and generous; but if you are selfish and try to slip away from everything that is unpleasant, you may at last come to commit some of the basest deeds such as make men infamous.

"*Resist beginnings*, all too late the cure,
  When ills have gathered strength by long delay."

"The greatest evils in life," we are reminded by Bishop Butler, "have had their rise from somewhat which was thought of too little importance to be attended to."

The very absence of crime and great sin which, if present, might have shocked us into repentance, may lull us into a sleep of fatal security and self-righteousness. To prevent this, let us adopt a high standard of Christian excellence, and endeavour to reach it by attention to small things. At this solemn season especially it becomes us to examine our characters, that we may by Christ's help put away those little sins which keep us from Him. If we do not do this in time, we may ruin ourselves for ever. How full of remorse then will be the reflection that

"It was the little rift within the lute
  That, ever widening, slowly silenced all;
 Or little pitted speck in garnered fruit
  That rotting inward slowly mouldered all."

Every one who is at all in the habit of self-examination must be conscious of such within him—indolence, vanity, ill-temper, weakness, yielding to the opinion and ridicule of the world, the temptation of bad passions, of which we are ashamed, but by which we are overcome. Let each of us consider what his peculiar infirmity is, and though the Zoar be a little one, and though it be hard to part with, resolutely determine to give it up to destruction.

Why did Lot desire to take refuge in Zoar? Because he was afraid of the consequences of obeying God's command. He did not know or believe that "because right is right, to follow right is wisdom in the scorn of consequences." His life in the plain, though surrounded by moral pollution, was comfortable, easy, and free from physical danger. He might have to endure hardness when he got up to the more bracing atmosphere of the mountain. What dangers awaited him there he knew not, and he had not that trust in God which makes the faithful willing to face the unknown future, with His rod and His staff to comfort them.

This is human nature, at least our human nature, for do not we shrink from giving up our sins because we dread and dislike the consequences of right-doing? A man is not quite honest in his business, because he fears that if he does not conform to the tricks of trade he will lose some of his customers, or at least his full share of profit. Another fears to become a decided Christian because he thinks that religion will put disagreeable restraints upon his conduct. He will have nothing to do with Jesus, lest He torment him. Another will not ascend the holy mountain, because it would be lonely for him to be away from his companions who live in the sinful cities of the plain. They would speak of him as eccentric and unsociable, and would even direct against him that most dreaded of weapons—"the coxcomb's argument of a grin."

For such reasons as these we beg for a Zoar to take refuge in. We are willing that the large sinful cities of the plain should be destroyed, but this little Zoar—" Is it not a little one?" To such pleadings God's answer is, " Escape for thy life ; look not behind thee, neither stay thou in all the plain ; escape to the mountain, lest thou be consumed."

You may desire very much to remain in Zoar with its comfort and old associations, and may almost despair of being able to leave it, but you can, if you will look to the hills, whence cometh your strength. Looking unto Jesus enables us to put away the sin that doth so easily beset us.

There is a military command " Eyes Right ! " and the Captain of our salvation gives the same in reference to the eyes of our soul. The right direction for the eyes of the soul is to look up and not look down, to look out and not look in, to look forward and not look backward. Look up to whatsoever things are honest, just, lovely, and of good report, and not down to whatsoever things are earthly, sensual, and devilish. Look out to the Great Healer, and not in on the wounds of sin. Look forward to victory over sin in the future, and not always back upon failure in the past.

Let us remember, that if ever we are to have a character capable of enjoying the mountain of holiness, we must not now despise the day of small things. Character is built, like the walls of an edifice, by laying one stone upon another. A mountain is ascended by setting one footstep after another up its steep face; if there be an occasional backward slip, a lesson of caution is learned, and the lost path is regained with determination. Holiness is not a rapture; it is a steady living to God, one step at a time, and every one higher up.

> "I count this thing to be grandly true—
>   That a righteous deed is a step towards God,
>   Lifting the soul from its common clod
> To a purer air and a clearer view.
>
> Heaven is not reached by a single bound;
>   Christ is the ladder by which we rise
>   From the lowly earth to the vaulted skies;
> And we mount to the summit round by round."

"How can you quiet your conscience by such sophistry?" asked a professor of religion of an atheist. "How can you quiet *yours?*" was the reply. "If I believed what you profess, I should think no zeal sufficient." The exponent of religion, living too near the world, contradicted his own arguments. The tempter tries sometimes to draw us with a hair, when we would resist a *rope:* we give way in some little thing, forgetting that our only strength is in cleaving wholly and utterly to the Rock of Ages. I heard of the keeper of a railway-bridge over a sheet of water who was entreated by a captain below, a friend of his own, to lift the bridge "just this once" for the passage of his ship. The railway servant argued that his duty was to retain the bridge in position till the express had passed, but he went on protesting and listening to his friend's persuasions, till at last he obliged him, "only this once." By this time other vessels had congregated, and having given way to one captain the pleadings of the others were granted likewise— the boats passed through, but on came the express, and ruin and loss of life were the result. "You think you will leave God's track this once and then return," was the rebuke of a clergyman to an inconsistent parishioner; "believe me, if you do, the return is very doubtful." In yielding to *one* temptation, the way is opened for so *many;* nothing will serve us day by day but a humble trust in Him who is able to keep us from falling, and earnest striving to put away those sins which we are too apt to cherish because "they are so little."

I believe it was St. Augustine who said, "God is great in great things, but greatest in the small"; and the more careful we are of the minutiæ of our conduct, the more do we resemble God.

XXI.

FOREWARNED, FOREARMED.

"Wherefore let him that thinketh he standeth take heed lest he fall."—1 COR. x. 12.

IN the beginning of this chapter, St. Paul reminds the Corinthians to whom he is writing that the people of Israel had religious privileges which might have been blessings if they had used them rightly, but which, being neglected or abused, did them more harm than good. Like Christians, the Jews had in their Church the sacrament of baptism and spiritual food. "They were all baptized unto Moses in the cloud and in the sea; and did all eat the same spiritual meat; and did all drink the same spiritual drink: for they drank of that spiritual Rock that followed them; and that Rock was Christ." Baptism is the solemn profession of our Christianity, as the passing through the Red Sea was the Israelite's profession of discipleship to Moses: then they passed the Rubicon, the die was cast, and thenceforward there was no return for them. One solemn step had severed them for ever from Egypt. "But with many of them God was not well pleased: for they were overthrown in the wilderness."

Having then established this parallel, the Apostle draws his conclusion. The Jews had as full privileges as you Corinthians have, and yet they fell. Be forewarned by their example, and do not think that you can escape by resting on religious privileges alone and without any effort on your parts. "Let him that thinketh he standeth take heed lest he fall."

It has been remarked that the men and women in the Bible whose fall from righteousness and their own good intentions has been recorded for our warning, fell just in that part of their characters which seemed most strong. Moses was the meekest of men, and yet he sinned unadvisedly with his lips. St. Peter was, as a rule, full of impulsive bravery, and yet for want of moral courage he denied his Lord. St. John was pre-eminently the apostle of love, but he it was who desired to call down fire from heaven against his enemies. Elijah was not afraid to rebuke a king to his face, but on one occasion he fell into such a fit of cowardly despondency that he asked God to take away his life. When a man commits some great sin or crime, his friends are often heard to say, "Well, I never would have thought of him doing that. He is the last man in the world to have done it." And that is just why he did it, because, like his friends, the man himself thought that he was quite safe from falling in that respect, and as a consequence he took no precaution against doing so.

Our subject, then, is the danger the best of us are in of falling into sin if we are not forearmed by being forewarned, and how much further a sin yielded to will carry us in the ways of wickedness than we thought at first that it would. In both these respects " let him that thinketh he standeth take heed lest he fall." A man was being served with a writ for debt. Knowing that if he got beyond the boundary of his county he could not be obliged to take a writ made out for another county, he being near the boundary line ran as hard as he could away from the bailiff, and escaped. On coming up to him the bailiff said, " You have given me a good run, and no mistake, but don't let us part enemies, let us shake hands." The man did so, and the bailiff pulled him over the fence and then arrested him. That is what sin does with us if we are not on our guard against it.

Let any one consider the character of the first and last temptation in a series of temptations. The first time the temptation occurs to us to commit some pleasant, but sinful act, there is a shudder and a horror and a feeling of impossibilty. "I cannot, cannot do it," we say. The next time the tempting thought comes to our mind it is treated with greater civility, it is a more welcome guest. We begin now to reason with it, instead of dashing it from us, which would have been the wisest course. Then we ask ourselves, is it really so bad after all? How can this be such a very great sin when, every day, thousands whom the world calls respectable commit it? At last the evil thought passes into the evil act, and the second transgression becomes easier by recollecting the facility and pleasantness of the first. We now shudder and are reluctant no longer, but plunge daily down the precipice on the brink of which we once trembled. All good to us is lost, evil has become our good. The power of habit "first draws, then drags, then hauls." That temptation which in the beginning was no stronger than a cobweb, was so strengthened by indulgence that it became a cable, and we were forced, in the words of Isaiah, to "draw iniquity with cords of vanity, and sin as it were with a cart rope."

This is every day illustrated by the liar and the drunkard. We know what horror the child who has been trained to love truth feels when first the temptation arises in his mind to shelter himself from punishment by telling a lie. "How can I do this great wickedness and sin against God?" If he yield to the temptation, he is ashamed and full of remorse because the brightness of his truthful soul has been tarnished by a first lie. And then when years of untruthfulness have passed over his head, he begins to consider a truthful man almost a fool, believing as he does that deceit and untruthfulness are the ordinary unavoidable means of gaining our ends in the world. At last he arrives at the liar's last stage, which is to believe his own lies.

Or take an illustration from the easy descent into the hell of drunkenness. Some of the most gifted of our race have been drunkards, and there are at present about 600,000 confirmed drunkards in Great Britain. Do you think they became drunkards the moment they tasted alcohol? No, the time was when many of them looked upon drunkenness with abhorrence and loathing. The first time they tasted intoxicating liquor as children they probably disliked it very much; but boys fancied that it was a manly thing to drink, and when they ceased to be boys they did not like to resist the apparent good fellowship of friendly glasses. Or some sorrow drove them to drown their senses in the drunkard's cup of forgetfulness. There is only one way by which any man ever became a drunkard, and that is by growing fond of alcohol, at first in moderate drinking—day by day a little increased, year by year a little multiplied by the solitary becoming the frequent, and the frequent the habitual, and the habitual the all-but-inevitable transgression.

> "We are not worst at once; the course of evil
> Begins so slowly and from such slight source,
> An infant's hand might stem the breach with clay:
> But let the stream grow wider, and philosophy,
> Ay and religion too, may strive in vain
> To stem the headlong current."

But indeed all sin approaches in the same gradual way. How easily, for instance, do self-indulgent habits come upon us, and how surely do they lead to great crimes. George Eliot gives in "Romola" the picture of a man, good, generous, handsome, with all the appliances and means of doing good, who, "because he tried to slip away from everything that was unpleasant, and cared for nothing so much as his own safety, came at last to commit some of the basest deeds such as make men infamous."

The holy man who exclaimed as he saw a criminal led to execution—"There goes me but for the grace of God," was not exaggerating, but only speaking from observation and experience. All men who know themselves are conscious that a bias towards evil exists within them. Daily experience teaches us that we are conceived in sin and shapen in iniquity, and that we can and do shape ourselves into further sin and ever-deepening iniquity if we neglect to make use of the means of counteracting our corrupt tendencies. When we see a man fall from the top of a five-story house, we say the man is lost. We say that before he has fallen a foot; for the same principle that made him fall one foot will undoubtedly make him complete the descent by falling other eighty or ninety feet. So that he is a dead man, or a lost man, from the very first. The gravitation of sin in a human soul acts precisely in the same way. Gradually, with gathering force, it sinks a man further and further from goodness, and lands him, by the action of a natural law, in the hell of a neglected life.

"O hold Thou up my goings in Thy paths: that my footsteps slip not." This is a needful prayer, for it is the first step towards sin that costs. We are weakened immeasurably from the instant that we have yielded to the tempter. One thread broken in the order of our virtue, we cannot tell how much of it will now unravel. St. James describes in three words the fearful gradation: "Earthly, sensual, devilish!" Earthly: that is, under the influence of the world, living only for business, for money, for pleasure; a mere earthworm, with nothing of the heavenly in our lives or in our hearts. That is the first step, but the next is worse. Sensual: living for fleshly gratification, pursuing carnal pleasure and sacrificing everything in the chase. Surely that is low enough. But we cannot stop there. We are on an incline, and we are not yet at the bottom. Down we go. Devilish: yes, for without the grace of God this is what we will become; His image completely effaced; even all that is man-like crushed out of us. Frightful degradation; and perhaps some of us are already on the steps. We ought to be careful, the gradient is steep! Sin plunges into ruin him who ceases to fight against it.

In the late Zulu and Afghanistan wars some of our forces suffered disaster, not because they were weak or cowardly, but because they felt so strong and brave that they thought they might be careless and off their guard in front of a despised enemy. That we may not make this mistake in our warfare against sin, "let him that thinketh he standeth take heed lest he fall."

But though it is wise in our passage over life's troublesome sea to distrust our own power of resisting the waves of temptation, let us never forget that these waves will be stilled, if, having Jesus in the boat with us, we cry unto Him for help. Once there was a little boy whose father was mate of a vessel, and as his ship was going to sea, he took his son along with him. A terrible storm arose, and the great waves rolled over the deck, and all the sailors were filled with terror, expecting every moment that the ship would spring a leak, and that they should lose their lives. While all was confusion and alarm, the little boy remained perfectly calm and fearless, to the utter astonishment of the crew; and when they asked him why he did not tremble at the danger, he looked at them with perfect composure and exclaimed, "My father is at the helm." Cannot we say the same?

XXII.

NO WASTE.

"Gather up the fragments that remain, that nothing be lost."
JOHN vi. 12.

THIS was the command which was given by our Lord to His disciples, when with only five loaves and two fishes He had fed five thousand men. Strange that He who could in this way multiply loaves should have been so particular about crumbs! And yet it will not appear strange if we reflect a little upon God's method of working in nature. In the material world as it has been arranged by Him there is no such thing as waste. Men who have studied science tell us that it is utterly impossible to destroy the least particle of matter. You tear up a letter, throw the pieces into the fire, and think that your letter is destroyed; but it is not. It has been changed into gases and other elements, but it has not been destroyed, and there is not the smallest diminution in the amount of matter in the world after it has been burnt. It is equally impossible to destroy force. One kind of force may be transformed into another, but there is not the slightest waste in the process. When giving this order, then, our Lord was, as always, showing to us the character and purpose of God. He was only acting in the spirit of His heavenly Father when He forbade waste and said, "Gather up the fragments that remain, that nothing be lost."

No doubt, too, He wished to teach that it is a duty to make the most of and put to the best account every gift of God. Nothing is more painfully sad to a thoughtful mind than to see people despising the blessings of God merely because they are common, and wasting His gifts if not required for immediate use, instead of keeping them until they are required. When Carlyle, the great writer, on his walks used to find a piece of bread thrown away by some careless person, he would get very indignant, pick it up and place it upon a house-step or other place where it could be easily seen, remarking that "some poor body might be glad of it, or at least a dog." If that man is to be regarded as a benefactor of his species who makes two stalks of corn to grow where only one grew before, not less is he or she to be regarded as a public benefactor who economizes and turns to the best practical account the food-products of human skill and labour.

This is one of the many lessons which may be learned from the command of Jesus; but assuredly food for our bodies is not the only kind of food which He forbids us to waste. His desire is that nothing should be lost of the nourishment He provides for our souls, and it cannot but grieve Him to see how we abuse or fail to use the means of grace and opportunities for serving Him which are more or less within reach of all of us.

"Gather up the fragments that remain, that nothing be lost." These words are full of hope and encouragement for us when we are saddened at the thought of what our lives are and of what they might be. Who can say that his life is as complete and perfect as God intended it to be, or as the man himself or his mother for him once hoped that it would be? "There is," says one, "in every child of man an ideal primitive being which nature has designed with her most maternal hand, but which man too often strangles or corrupts." "From what have I not fallen," writes another, "if the child which I remember was indeed myself." Is there any man of middle age who can say that he has kept the promise of his childhood, or who fails to see the truth of Jeremy Taylor's eloquent words when he compares the beginning of life to a young trooper riding into battle blithe and gay, in all the bravery of soul and dress, and its end to the same soldier riding back—weary, and stained, and wounded—a defeated and shattered man?

> " How like a younker, or a prodigal,
> The scarfèd bark puts from her native bay,
> Hugged and embraced by the strumpet wind ;
> How like a prodigal does she return
> With over-wreathed ribs and ragged sails,
> Lean, rent, and beggared by the strumpet wind."

No one is as happy or as good as he might have been, and he must indeed have had very low ideals who can say that he had realized them.

But though our lives are in many respects broken and unsatisfactory, mere fragments of what lives should be, we must not despair. We are disobedient to the spirit of Christ's command if we do not strive with all our ability to gather up the fragments that remain and make the most of them. Let us suppose the case of a man who has lost his health and become a chronic invalid. He may act in either of two ways. He may grumble through life and despair of doing anything because ill-health appears to have cut him off from happiness and usefulness ; or he may see in his affliction the hand of a heavenly Father, and seeing this may resolve to make the most of the blessings that still remain to him in life. How nobly the late Postmaster-General did this last when he was afflicted with the terrible loss of sight at twenty-two years of age. On being brought home after the fatal shot had ruined his eyes, Professor Fawcett was in utter despair. The prospects of realizing his ambitious plans seemed shattered, and for weeks he remained in a state of utter collapse. At last he was roused to energy by the wise letter of a friend which pointed out some of the duties and even pleasures that were open to the blind, and he resolved to do and be all that he had purposed doing and being before the accident. And so well did he succeed, that it was sometimes said of him that he "never saw until he became blind." The other day I read of one who had great talent for painting, which seemed at first to be in danger of being wasted by the loss of the use of both of his hands. Nothing daunted, the brave artist continued to paint beautiful pictures holding the brush with his teeth. He gathered up the fragments that remained.

Sometimes a man feels that his life is marred because he has got into some profession or business which does not suit him. What is he to do? Is he to do his work in a careless, half-hearted way; or is he not much rather to make the most of uncongenial circumstances, gathering up the fragments of his broken career and consecrating them to God?

"Gather up the fragments that remain," says our Saviour in reference to time and in reference to opportunities of serving Him. God knows we have lost all too much of time or the stuff of which our lives are made. The hours pass and are put to our account, but when young we think nothing of this. We speak of killing time, as if it were an enemy to be got rid of, instead of a possession so valuable that one day we will be ready to give all that we possess for a moment of it. "Have you ever seen those marble statues in some public square or garden, which art has so fashioned into a perennial fountain that through the lips or through the hands the clear water flows in a perpetual stream, on and on for ever; and the marble stands there—passive, cold—making no effort to arrest the gliding water." We are like these marble statues, all unconscious of the fact that time is passing through our hands. Christ would also have us to obey this command of His in reference to the opportunities of usefulness that still remain to us. Each one of us has been put into the world for a definite purpose, in order that we might make the little corner in which we are placed better and brighter. Then we have all been given the power of more or less influencing others for good. We have had, too, our own hearts to cultivate by deeds of love. We might have made our home almost a heaven by kind words and thoughtful attentions. We might have helped to feed the lambs and sheep of Christ's flock. We might have soothed the sufferings of hundreds. Surely we cannot think back on the opportunities we have missed of doing these things without a feeling of shame and remorse, and a firm resolve to make the most of any opportunities of a like kind that a merciful God may graciously give us. If the thought comes into our minds that it is too late, and that we can hope to do no good now either for ourselves or for others, let us banish it in the Saviour's name. If we have lived lives useless and perhaps injurious to others, all the more reason that now we should gather up whatever opportunities of undoing evil and of doing good still remain. Our past has been foolish, frivolous, perhaps disgraceful; but Christ says, My servant, be sad but do not despair. Though the feast of life has in your case been wasted, yet there are fragments that remain, and these I would have you to gather up. If there is any one this Lent who hears the voice of Jesus speaking thus to his heart, let him no longer delay. One more chance is given to you—use it, for it may be the last. Use it, or, if you do not, over your soul will creep the chill of a more fatal apathy, and then for you the words of the text will have to be altered, not saying as Christ said to His faithful ones, " Gather up the fragments that remain, that nothing be lost," but rather, alas! with a more urgent insistency, " Gather up the fragments that remain, lest everything be lost."

How differently we see different men act when by some error or even crime they have fallen in life. One is no sooner down than he begins to think of getting up again, rebounding like a ball to the position from which he had fallen. Another thinks that all is lost, makes no effort, and, as a consequence, sinks lower and lower. An American gentleman, when talking to me of the dogged perseverance of his nation, gave as an instance the case of his own father. "My father," he said, " failed in business six times, and then made a large fortune." On expressing my surprise that a man could do this in these days of keen competition, the American used words which I have never forgotten. "You don't know," he said, "the kind of man my father was. He was a man who would never stay broken." My brethren, if it be possible to display this zeal, courage, and indomitable will in the pursuit of riches that are only enjoyed for five or ten years, ought we not to determine never to stay broken, even if over and over again we have become bankrupt, of the riches of Christ that endure for ever? If we have allowed the chain of bad habits to become so tight that we almost despair of ever escaping from its degrading bondage; if our lives are base, unworthy, and so incomplete that they are mere fragments of what they might be and ought to be—if this be our case, what are we going to do? Are we going to stay broken? or shall we not rather take the wretched remnants of our used-up selves and give them to that Saviour who, in the greatness of His love, will accept them and put them, even thus late in the day, to a good account? Be sure that He who was careful of broken pieces of bread is not indifferent to a broken and contrite heart. Let us remember for our encouragement how, when He was on earth, He laboured among the guilty; how He associated with outcasts in order to save them; how tenderly and lovingly He used to speak to those whom society counted undone; how He loved to bind up the bruised and the broken-hearted; how His breath fanned the spark which seemed dying out in the wick of the expiring taper, when men thought that it was too late, and that the hour of hopeless depravity had come.

The mistake many make, is trying to gather up the fragments of their broken lives in their own strength without thinking of the only One who can enable them to do it. Here is an instance that was brought to my notice. During the Crimean war a man who had a very bad character enlisted in the army. So often had he been before the magistrate for drunkenness, that that gentleman, on his coming before him to be attested, was so glad at the prospect of getting rid of him, that he gave him ten shillings and said that he hoped never to see him again. The man lost a leg in one of the battles, and on coming out of hospital was induced by the example of a comrade to sign the total abstinence pledge, and he did it in a way which at least proved that he was very much in earnest about it. He scratched his arm, and with the blood that issued out signed the pledge. Less than a week afterwards he was drunk, his own blood not being able to save him. Happily he was pointed to blood that can save from sin, became a penitent disciple of Jesus Christ, and, on returning to his village after the war, was so altered for the better, that the very magistrate who gave him ten shillings to express his joy at seeing what he thought would be the last of him, took him into his service, even though he had a limb less; and there he was living years afterwards

NO WASTE.

when last I heard of him. This man found that he could not gather up the fragments that remained of his almost ruined life in his own strength; but he was enabled to do so by the precious blood of Jesus: and so shall we if, looking only to Him, we make the attempt.

> " O patient watcher over all !
> If broken lives may best complete
> Thy circle, let our fragments fall
> An offering at thy feet."

XXIII.

GOOD FRIDAY AND BAD FRIDAY.

"Thus it is written, and thus it behoved Christ to suffer, and to rise from the dead the third day: And that repentance and remission of sins should be preached in His name among all nations, beginning at Jerusalem."—LUKE xxiv. 46, 47.

ONE of the seven last sayings of our Saviour when He was being tortured on the bitter cross for us men and for our salvation, was a prayer for His murderers—"Father, forgive them, for they know not what they do." And, brethren, He was acting in the same spirit when, after having risen from the dead, He appeared to His disciples and told them that remission or pardon of sin on condition of repentance should be preached in His name to all nations, and that this gracious message should first of all be proclaimed at Jerusalem.

At Jerusalem, of all places in the world! There could not possibly be a greater proof of forgiving love than this. If Jerusalem sinners could be saved on condition of repentance, no one need despair. It was this thought which brought comfort to John Bunyan when he was deep down in the Slough of Despond about his sins, and caused him to write that wonderful discourse which has given hope to many, called "Grace Abounding to the Chief of Sinners."

On this Good Friday, brethren, if we measure our sins not by the standard of public opinion or by comparing them with those of our neighbours, but by the lurid light shed on them by the cross of Christ, we cannot but come to the conclusion that we are the chief of sinners.

Well, then, grace abounds to us, for whatever we are, we are not worse than the sinners of Jerusalem to whom it was commanded that the message of forgiveness should first be proclaimed.

In Jerusalem lived the actual murderers of the Just One, and if those who crucified the Son of God and put Him to an open shame were to have the gospel preached to them first, the extent of the forgiving love of Jesus must indeed be immeasurable. "At Jerusalem!" Is it possible? Why, that is where Judas betrayed his Lord with a kiss and sold Him who came to set us free for thirty pieces of silver, the price of a slave! At Jerusalem, where Pilate, after publicly declaring that he could find no fault in Christ, ordered Him to be crucified, in order to please a blood-thirsty mob. At Jerusalem, where Peter denied Him for fear of the words of a little servant-girl, and where the cowardly disciples were when they forsook him and fled. At Jerusalem, where the chief priests, elders, and scribes desired to kill Him to gratify their envy, and moved the easily-led multitude to ask that Barabbas the robber should be spared rather than Him who did no sin, and in whose mouth there was no guile. At Jerusalem, where the fickle multitude so quickly altered their shouts from "Hosanna!" to "Crucify Him." At Jerusalem, where many bore false witness against Him; where they that passed by railed on Him; where the soldiers smote Him with a reed and with their hands, spat on Him and put on His head a crown of thorns. At Jerusalem, where Herod set Him at nought and mocked Him with his men of war. Certainly the day may well be called "Good Friday" which commemorates forgiving love like this. In ancient times the day was called "The Day of the Cross," "The Pasch of the Cross," "The Great Preparation," and the like; but no name is so beautiful and so appropriate as that by which it is now known—"Good Friday."

And yet from another point of view the day might well be called "Bad Friday," the worst that ever dawned, for then was perpetrated the greatest crime and the darkest tragedy revealed in history. And it was our sins that did it. That is to say, it was sins of the very same kind which we commit, which once came to a crisis, so to speak, in the crucifixion of Incarnate Goodness. It was thus that the Saviour

looked on the sins of His day. The Jews of that
day had had no hand in the murder of Abel or Zach-
arias; but they were of kindred spirit with the men
who slew them. They condemned, no doubt, the
murderers of these men, but they imitated their act.
In that imitation they "allowed the deeds of their
fathers;" they shared in the guilt of the act which
had been consummated, because they had the spirit
which led to it. In the same way our sins may be
said to have crucified the Son of God, for we act in
our day in the same spirit as those people did in
theirs who brought about the death of Jesus.

We think that Judas was acting in a terribly wicked
way when he betrayed Jesus; but so are we when we
are false to our friends. When we are placed in
positions of responsibility, do we never advocate a
policy of selfish expediency, as Caiaphas did? Are
we never weak and unjust like Pilate; moral cowards
like Peter; cruel like those who mocked the sufferings of Jesus; lovers of evil men rather than of good
like those who cried "Not this man, but Barabbas?"
When we think with horror on the crime of those
who crucified the Just One, let us ask ourselves, If we
had lived then, on which side would we have been?
Would we have cried "Crucify Him," or would we,
like Joseph of Arimathæa, have not consented to the
counsel and deed of His enemies?

Be sure, brethren, that if we are not on the side of
Christ now, we would not have been had we lived
when He was in the flesh on this earth. If we are

not on His side now, we are certain every day to be committing the same sort of sins as those did who crucified the Just One. Let us not, then, make light of sin, for the measure of the guilt and blackness of sin is the cross of Christ. We shudder at the wickedness of Judas, but we ought to reflect that it was our sins no less than his treachery which caused the death of our Lord, and that each time we voluntarily give way to our besetting sin, whether it be covetousness, cowardice, injustice, cruelty, or any other temptation, we wilfully share the guilt and incur the danger of our Lord's betrayers and murderers. If Christ were now to come to London instead of to Jerusalem, and in a way that He could not easily be identified, what would we do with Him? What we do to every one now who tries to live above the maxims and practices of the world, and who both by rebuke and example disturbs us in our pleasant vices.

Never before or since did the powers of darkness contend in such deadly strife with the powers of light as when they crucified our Redeemer. We cannot but be touched and grieved when we read the four accounts that are given by the Evangelists of our Lord's Passion. It is said that a poor ignorant old woman, who had been reading in her New Testament the account of the tragedy commemorated on Good Friday, said to her clergyman who happened to visit her soon afterwards, " Reading about that cruel death, sir, has made me so sad; but it all happened so long ago that we must hope it is not true."

Instead of hoping that it is not true, let us believe that it is true, and then there will be peace and beauty in our lives—Christ's peace and beauty. The history of the death of Jesus is as sad to any thoughtful mind as it was to the poor old woman; but there is another side to it which speaks of hope and reconciliation. The self-sacrifice of Christ manifests and proves to us, as nothing else could, that God loves us in spite of our sins; that He respects us when we have lost the respect of men and even our own self-respect. If anything can soften and melt our hard hearts, it is love like this. We give up all attempts to justify and excuse ourselves. We confess that we are sinners and unworthy of such love. And then as we feel that God is our loving Father, the dutiful and affectionate feelings which children ought to feel rise up in us. Giving up all hard and unworthy thoughts of God, we that were sometimes alienated and enemies in our mind by wicked works can say "Our Father," and not only say the words but feel their meaning, for we have been reconciled.

But not only does the death of Jesus atone or put at one man and God; it also reconciles man and man, and man to the duties of his life. Through Christ man is reconciled to man, "For He is our peace, who hath made both one, and hath broken down the middle wall of partition between us." In Christ, all "people, nations, and languages" are brothers; for they can all point to Him as their Elder Brother and the Head of their common humanity. He is the Head of all, for all have sinned and come short of the glory of God—are we not, then, brothers in guilt and brothers in redemption? Statesmen and politicians believe that men may be united by self-interest—by considering their common advantage in maintaining peace; but surely the cross of Christ or the spirit of self-sacrifice is a "more excellent way." "No man for himself, every man for all," is the motto which the life and death of Jesus reveals as the true uniting power of nations, churches, families, and individuals. The spirit of the Cross is the spirit of denying ourselves, our own desires and prejudices, for others; and what can unite man to man but this mutual forbearance and mutual toleration?

Lastly, Christ reconciles each of us to the duties of our position in life. There are many who fancy that they are not properly placed in the world. Their trades and professions, it may be, do not appear suited to them. Perhaps their lives are dull, and they desire a more exciting, active position. They are called upon to suffer much misery, and even when no great calamity afflicts them the little trials and burdens of every-day life are never absent. Let them look to the life and death of Christ, and the mystery of their lives becomes plain. They will become reconciled to their lives and duties by endeavouring to live in the spirit of Him who reconciled the life of God with the lowly duties of a servant.

XXIV.

THE FULL, PERFECT, AND SUFFICIENT SACRIFICE.

" Verily, verily, I say unto you, Except a corn of wheat fall into the ground and die, it abideth alone: but if it die, it bringeth forth much fruit."—JOHN xii. 24.

IN these words our Lord represents His own sacrifice as parallel with that great law of self-sacrifice which runs through all nature. As the corn of wheat cannot bring forth fruit except it die, so Christ could only save others by dying and not saving Himself.

No law of nature is more mysterious nor any more universal than this—that whoever or whatever saves others cannot save themselves. Let us take some familiar examples of this law of others being saved by sacrifice—of life springing out of death. Has not the deer to die that the tiger may live? What is the meaning of the timid cry of the small birds when they hover round the hawk as the moth hovers round the candle? Is not the whole of nature "red in tooth and claw"? Do not soldiers pass on to victory over the bodies of their comrades who die in order that they may triumph? Nay, are we not reminded of this law of life from death every time we sit down to dinner and eat of those animals by the death of which we live? Are not too nearly all the luxuries, pleasures, and even necessities of our lives procured by the sweat of another's brow and by the toil of another's hands?

Now in all such instances the law of self-sacrifice is obeyed unconsciously or instinctively. Not so, however, when our Saviour voluntarily submitted to it "for us men and for our salvation." Consciously, and with full power either to take it up or to lay it down, He sacrificed His life, and by doing so submitted His will to God's. His sacrifice consisted in recognizing this universal law of self-sacrifice as the will of God, and in voluntarily submitting to it. Foreseeing what the result of His steady opposition to the world's sin would be, He persevered even unto death, battling against it in all its forms; and this it is which prevents His death from being merely that of a struggling lamb dragged to the altar, and elevates it to the dignity of a true because voluntary sacrifice. His death was the joyful surrender of His will to God's. " Wherefore when he cometh into the world He saith, Sacrifice and offering Thou wouldest not. In burnt offerings and sacrifices for sin Thou hast no pleasure. Then said I, Lo I come (in the volume of the book it is written of me), to do Thy will, O God."

All speculations as to why Christ should have to suffer for us are unprofitable and useless so long as we only "know in part." No answer to our questions about the why of the atonement can be given until we are enabled to solve that greater mystery of which it forms a part—namely, the origin and continuance of sin and suffering in God's world concerning which

> "What hope of answer or redress?
> Behind the veil, behind the veil."

Unhappily, however, those who would be wise above that which is written, are not content to simply accept for their soul's comfort the fact that Christ died for them. They vainly speculate and form theories as to why He did so, none of which are at all reliable, and some are of such a sort as to present stumbling-blocks to the acceptance of Christianity on the part of many good and spiritually-minded men.

The common theory is that God's justice demanded a victim, and that an innocent one would do as well as another. But we may ask, Is this justice? or is it not the case that if we men acted on such justice in our law courts and in the affairs of life generally, the very idea of justice would soon be lost? "The soul that sinneth, it shall die," is surely the voice of conscience. Nor should we ascribe acts of injustice to God which we would not to a good man, and then say that we are not to judge of God's justice from our own; for there is nothing else from which we can judge of God's justice, goodness, and other attributes, except from the justice and goodness which we find in those around us and in ourselves. But indeed this subject is far too full of mystery, by reason of our scanty knowledge, for anything like dogmatism concerning it. It is wiser far, considering how very ignorant we are of the whole matter, not to speak of justice or injustice in reference to it. When our Lord met His disciples as they journeyed to Emmaus, and opened their understanding that they might understand the Scriptures, He did not give them any theory of why He suffered, nor did He enter into any explanation as to the justice of God. Saying nothing at all of the why, He simply declared the fact that "Thus it is written, and thus it behoved Christ to suffer and to rise from the dead the third day"; and then what most of all concerned them, " that repentance and remission of sins should be preached in His name to all nations."

Most people, it is to be hoped, have ceased to speak of the atonement as it used to be spoken of. Some there were who seemed to believe that there were two Gods—One God the Father, a revengeful, bloodthirsty Deity, from whom we had to be sheltered by another, God the Son. Of course these persons did not acknowledge such a distinction even to themselves, but their language practically pointed to it.

Let us, however, remember that it was God Himself who, in His assumed human nature, died for us, and there will be no room for such a horrible view as that which represents the loving God so full of rage as to be indifferent on whose head His blow should fall. Let us ever remember that in some mysterious way, unexplained by Scripture, God's victim was Himself, and then we shall not represent Him in terms which well describe the ungoverned rage of Saul missing his stroke at David who has offended, and in disappointed fury dashing his javelin at his son Jonathan; but which do not well describe this inexplicable miracle of love and mercy, that the all-powerful God, instead of crushing us sinners, should come down from heaven to die for us in order that we might have proof of His loving kindness towards us, and so be won from sin and selfishness to Himself and righteousness. We must not, in a pagan way, represent God's character as bloody, from which we have to be sheltered; but rather as that of a loving Father who never did desire, and desireth not now, the death of a sinner, but rather that he may turn from his wickedness, and live. God, who hateth nothing that He hath made, does not hate sinners though He hates their sins, and always will hate them—yes, and will purge them out of them by punishment, not in anger, but for the sake of sinners themselves. Oh, brethren, let not our selfishness acquiesce in the atonement as an ingenious scheme for saving us from punishment, and enabling us to live with impunity while we do not touch our cross with one of our fingers. Whoever can acquiesce in the thought, "Christ has suffered, I am safe; He bore the agony, I take the reward," chiefly in reference to personal safety, and, without desiring to share his Saviour's cross, aspire to enjoy the comforts and benefits of His Sacrifice, has in him that selfish spirit which takes all and gives nothing—the very opposite spirit to His, who said "It is more blessed to give than to receive."

Let us, then, form no theory as to the atonement, but with heartfelt gratitude accept the blessed fact that "God so loved the world that He gave His only begotten Son, that whosoever believeth in Him should not perish, but have everlasting life." For all theories on the subject tend to weigh down Christianity by rendering it responsible for the objections which may justly be brought against them. And indeed such theories are quite useless, for the practical part of this doctrine is what alone we have to do with, and concerning this all parties are agreed.

What, then, is the practical part which concerns us? First of all, Christ's cross, from whatever point of view we contemplate it, proclaims as nothing else could that God is love. It furnishes an answer, not certainly one which we can understand; but one which we can trust and receive strength from to the questions, Why do we suffer? Why have we such strong temptations and so little power to resist them? Why do the wicked prosper upon the earth? Why, in a word, are there so many dark and unintelligible mysteries of sorrow in God's world? It answers all such questions by telling us simply to have faith in God, to wait His time and to ask no more. Christ died, not to alter God's will, but to fulfil it : not to satisfy God's anger, but to manifest His love ; and therefore the cross proclaims that sin and suffering, however they have got into this world, are contrary to God's will; that He hates evil, and is doing all He can to root it out, though He may well be patient and act slowly, since He is eternal. For what more could even God do for His vineyard than send that Son in whom He was well pleased to die for it ?— and this we believe He did.

Then, too, every one of us individually may look to the cross and learn that God loves and does not hate even the most sinful of us, in spite of our past sins and errors. To miserable sinners whom thoughts of their long-lost innocency, of their sins committed against God, themselves, and their fellow-men are maddening, this message of love is sent to say, Forget the past, think only of the present and the future. Looking away from yourselves altogether — from your childhood's innocency, from your past sins and present feelings, to the cross of Christ, take courage from this revelation of God's love to try again. God loved us miserable sinners with such unselfish, practical love, that there was nothing He would not suffer for us—this is the message of the cross, which too often appears " foolishness " to us, so long as we are comfortable and prosperous, lazy and selfish. Then we shrink from the thought of Christ on His cross, which tells us that better men than we have had to suffer, that the Son of God Himself had to suffer. And we do not like suffering and trouble for the sake of duty; we prefer easy-going respectability. The careless selfish man shrinks from the sight of Christ on His cross, for it rebukes his carelessness and selfishness. It says to him, " You are base so long as you care for none of these things and only for yourself. Rise up, do something for your Saviour ; be of use, face discomfort, loss of worldly advantage, if it must be, for the sake of speaking truth and doing right. If you will not do as much as that, then no matter how great your reputation may be, the poorest woman who, unknown and unnoticed by all, sacrifices her ease and takes trouble for the sake of simple duties and little kindnesses, is more noble and more God-like than you."

That, brethren, is what the cross of Christ preaches to us, and we do not like it. We turn from it and say, We would hear smoother things, and prefer being told, what indeed is quite untrue, that Christ has left us nothing to do and no cross to bear ; that the path of duty is not rough and thorny, but comfortably paved and strewn with flowers. Why not

> " Smooth down the stubborn text to ears polite,
> And snugly keep (our duties) out of sight ? "

Such, brethren, is our language as long as the fine weather lasts, and all is bright. But when the tempest comes, when poverty, affliction, anxiety, shame, sickness, bereavement come, when we try to speak truth and find, as men often do, that speaking truth and doing right bring a remuneration which is not always agreeable in this world, then indeed the cross begins to mean something to us. In our misery we look up to Heaven and ask, Does God care for my trouble? Does He understand what it means? When men "daily mistake my words," and when "all they imagine is to do me evil," have I a Heavenly Father to whom I may appeal? Or must I fight the battle of life alone, without sympathy or help from God who made me! Then does the cross of Christ say to us as nothing else could, God does understand and feel with you, for Christ does so. Christ has suffered all this before you. He, the Son of God, endured poverty, fear, persecution, death for you, that He might be touched with the feeling of your infirmities, and that by considering Him that endured such contradiction of sinners against Himself, you might not be wearied and might not faint in your minds.

XXV.

VOLUNTEER FOR GOD.[1]

"If any man will do His will, he shall know of the doctrine, whether it be of God."—JOHN vii. 17.

WE meet to-day to celebrate Easter, the Queen of Festivals. Christmas has been called the "Mother of all Festivals," because it is the beginning and origin of all; but Easter is the "Queen of Feasts," because it crowns and completes them all. It is the great day of distinctive religious joy in the sense of the conquest of sin and death. The Pasch-egg, the symbol of life out of what seemed dead; the salutation, "Christ is risen," of Eastern custom; the early practice of freeing slaves and ransoming captives—all show how from time immemorial Easter has been the great festival of Christian hope and love.

[1] Preached to Volunteers and Soldiers on Easter Sunday.

"Christ is risen from the dead; and become the first-fruits of them that slept."

The first-fruits of the harvest were dedicated to God, whereby He put in His claim for the whole, just as shutting up a road once a year puts in a claim of proprietorship to the right of way for ever. It was thus St. Paul understood the ceremony: "For if the first-fruits be holy, the lump is also holy." Thus when the Apostle says that "Christ is the first-fruits of them that slept," he implies that part of the harvest has been claimed for God, and therefore that the rest is His too. The resurrection of Christ is a pledge of the resurrection of all who share in His humanity.

And Christ's resurrection is the chief proof as well as the central fact of our religion. The existence of the Christian Church, and its extension over the civilized world, are facts which we cannot account for unless we believe that Christ did really rise from the dead and put new hearts into His followers, so that they preferred deaths of torture rather than deny their risen Lord. Little capable were the disciples of founding a church on the night of their Master's betrayal, when one denied Him, and they all forsook Him and fled. Something must have happened to have changed these men so much that the scourgings of magistrates and the brutality of mobs could not prevent them from teaching in the name of Jesus, filling Jerusalem with their doctrine, and generally turning the world upside down. If Christ rose from the dead, all is explained; if He did not, the Church must have perished in the bud. People would not have listened to the apostles if they had no more to say than that their Master was put to a death as disgraceful as hanging is with us. The fact that Jesus was crucified between two thieves would have been an insuperable difficulty if this Jesus who, until the third day after His death must have seemed a failure, had not, as a matter of fact, been declared to be the Son of God with power by His resurrection. The Gospel of the resurrection was the only satisfactory explanation of the apparently disgraceful death of Him who seemed to be able to save neither Himself nor others.

Now Christ crucified is the chief topic of sermons, and the "offence of the cross" has ceased, but the earliest preachers of our religion had to put the resurrection of Jesus rather than His crucifixion in the foreground of their teaching. If they could not have triumphantly pointed to His resurrection their preaching would have been in vain. From a mistaken view of the writings of the Apostle Paul, as when he said, "I preach Christ crucified," it has been inferred that the chief doctrine he taught was the crucifixion; but it was the crucified and *risen* Saviour that he preached, rather than the mere fact of the crucifixion. To the Athenians he seemed to be a setter forth of strange gods, because he preached unto them Jesus and the resurrection. If the Apostle Peter went forth to proclaim the Gospel to the Jews, even before the Sanhedrim and before all the people, this was his doctrine, "Jesus and the Resurrection." Indeed, one of the chief qualifications for apostleship was to be able to bear witness to the reality of Christ's resurrection.

It is true that there are many difficulties connected with the fragmentary history of our Lord's resurrection which is given by the Evangelists; but there are many more difficulties in accounting for the rise and spread of the Christian religion, if we suppose that the apostles who bore witness to His resurrection and sealed this testimony with their blood were false or even mistaken witnesses.

The nature of things excludes such truths as the resurrection of Jesus from being demonstrated and verified; but, if probability is "the guide of life," there is quite enough evidence to justify us in believing it to be historically true. Certainly those who are indifferent or hostile to all that it implies, may resist the force of any argument that can be urged in favour of it. If, on the other hand, any man will, that is, wishes to do God's will, he shall know of the doctrine, whether it be of God. The landscape is only beautiful to those who bring to the sight of it the power of admiring, and the arguments for Christ's resurrection are only convincing to those who seek to rise with Christ above this world and their own selves. Not always, but very often, men think in a certain mode on these matters, because their life is of a certain character, and their opinions are in many cases invented afterwards as a defence for their life.

St. Paul speaks of a maxim among the Corinthians, "Let us eat and drink, *for* to-morrow we die." They excused their voluptuousness on the ground of its consistency with their sceptical creed. Life was short; death came to-morrow. There was no hereafter, and, being consistent, they would not live for one. Was not this creed the result rather than the cause of their life? Did they not *first* eat and drink, and *then* believe that they would die to-morrow? "Getting and spending, we lay waste our powers." Living only to eat and drink, we lose sight of the life to come. When the immortal is overborne and smothered in the life of the flesh, how *can* men believe in the life to come? Then disbelieving, we mistake the cause for the effect. Our habits and creed are in perfect consistency, and very often, though by no means always, it is the life that forms the creed. To sensualists, immortality is incredible.

Voluntariness is an element of success in everything, and, as the text teaches, it is especially applicable to religion. We honour our volunteers because they are willing to defend their country, and spare no trouble to prepare themselves for doing so. They shoot well, because they do not go through their rifle practice in a perfunctory way, but liking it and wishing to excel. Let them also volunteer or be willing to serve God, and they shall know of the doctrine.

If a man volunteer for God as Isaiah did when he said, "Here am I, send me;" or Samuel when he said, "Speak, for thy servant heareth"—if in this way a man is willing to serve God, he will not long remain in doubt about either his duty or his creed. Perhaps some of you, brethren, are called upon to work in large workshops where you hear opinions of all kinds expressed. You may be told that secularism is the highest and best gospel for working men, and that your salvation consists in living without God in the world, and rejecting the message of Good Friday and Easter Sunday. You are puzzled with conflicting opinions, and sometimes in despair, you ask with Pilate, " What is truth ? " In such an hour what remains ? I reply, Obedience. Leave those thoughts for the present. Act—be kind, gentle, sober, and honest; be true and just in all your dealings; try to do good to others; obey the duty you know. *That* must be right, whatever else is uncertain. By all the laws of the human heart, by the Word of God, you shall not be left to doubt. Do that much of the will of God which is plain to you, and "you shall know of the doctrine, whether it be of God." Pilate did not "stay for an answer" to his question, "What is truth ? " He was not in earnest, and did not deserve an answer. If we are in earnest, we shall persevere like the Syrophenician woman, " Even though the ear of the universe seems dead, and Christ Himself appear to bid us back."

In ancient times, Christians all over the world began Easter Day with a morning salutation. Each man said to his neighbour, " Christ is risen ; " and his neighbour answered him, " Christ is risen indeed, and hath appeared unto Simon!" Even to Simon, the coward disciple who denied him thrice, Christ is risen; even to us, who often vowed to obey Him, and have yet so often denied Him before men, so often taken part with sin, when He called us another way. "Christ is risen indeed, and hath appeared to Simon!" Shall we not endeavour once more to rise with him to newness of life. Let us volunteer to do so, and He will teach us His doctrine, and enable us to practise it in our lives; and then, when the short but stern battle of life is over, through the grave and gate of death we shall pass to our joyful resurrection. Amen.

XXVI.

THE LORD AND GIVER OF LIFE.

"He that hath the Son hath life; and he that hath not the Son of God hath not life."—1 JOHN V. 12.

IF religion had nothing to do with this present life, it would be enough to become religious when we are on the point of departing from life, when we are on the borders of another world; but it is never thus that the Bible speaks of religion. Rather it tells us that religion has the promise of this world as well as of that which is to come, that it is not a mere death-bed ornament, but something that beautifies, elevates, and makes noble this present life. Without it a man cannot live the highest life of which he is capable. There may be existence without religion, but not the sort of life which his Creator intended man to live. This being the case, we are not surprised to find that the text speaks of religion as something that we should have in our present life. It does not say he that hath the Son *shall* have life, but he that hath the Son *hath* life. As the oak is contained in the acorn, so eternal life has its seed and first beginnings in the life we are living now.

What life, even the life of the body, is in itself, we do not know. We only know it by its effects. One moment it is present, and a man can move, speak, think and love; another moment, and he is dead clay. We cannot explain what has taken place. Life is gone—that is all, but what a difference! But though unable to explain what life is, we feel that the more of it we have the better.

> "'Tis life, not death, for which we pant,
> More life and fuller that we want."

A man complains of a place that it has not enough life in it, and is tempted to engage in gambling, money speculation, dissipation, anything for more and fuller life.

Now the text tells us of One who can supply this universal craving. "He that hath the Son hath life." What is meant here by life? It means that spiritual, heavenly life, whereby we live to God and enjoy peace with Him; for to be carnally minded is death, but to be spiritually minded is life and peace. And this highest life of man is not measured by days, months, or years.

> "We live in deeds, not years; . . .
> He most lives who thinks most, feels the noblest, acts the best."

Sometimes a life of promise seems to us to be cut off too soon. A young man, richly endowed as regards intellect and power of usefulness, is taken away by death. This seems very hard and unintelligible. But suppose that young man, during his short stay upon earth, had given his heart to God; had kept his thoughts high and his feelings pure, had striven to serve man and to glorify God— might not he have lived in a very few years a really longer life than another who should drag out a selfish, purposeless, mean existence for a great number of years? He lives the longest life who puts his life to the best account. This, I suppose, is what the prophet Isaiah meant when he said, "The child shall die a hundred years old; but the sinner being a hundred years old shall be accursed."

Having seen what is meant by the life sopken of in the text, let us go on to consider the meaning of having the Son, which is to give us that life. It seems to mean, in the first instance, having the revelation which God gave by His Son. God taught us, through Jesus Christ, that sin is a very terrible thing, so terrible that it cost the death of the Son of God; but He did not stop here, He proved to us at the same time His great love to us sinners. And does not this revelation, when it is not merely a vague intellectual conception, or an article of the creed only on our lips, but a realization in the heart, put new life into us?

When a man looks back on his past life and sees that it has been, in almost every respect, what it ought not to have been, when he knows that his present life is depraved and therefore unhappy, when the future has no hope, as he thinks, for him, what can raise him from this deadness in trespasses and sin? Let him once realize that the revelation made by Jesus Christ is true for him personally, and a new life will be communicated to his soul from the Lord and Giver of life. He has the Son now, and therefore, he realizes the fact that he has a share of the life, spiritual, regenerate, eternal, which Christ promised to His faithful disciples when He said, "I am come that they might have life, and that they might have it more abundantly."

A true Christian is one who lives a double life, the ordinary life which all men live, and an inner, secret life which is hid with Christ in God. This life is the scene, so to speak, of his greatest joys and sorrows, and Christ is a sharer of both. He is the Head, and each true believer one of His members. He is the vine, and we are His branches, and we are strong, healthy, and fruitful, only by deriving sap and nourishment from the vine. The President of the United States may be very anxious to telegraph some important communication to the English Government in London, but he cannot do so if there is a break in the submarine wire. The wire is got up, the connection made complete, and then the electric current can flash messages as before. In the same way we cease to have any power in our inner life when we disconnect it with Him in whom is life. Again and again, as sin disconnects, we must try to get into communication once more. The life which Christ gives us often gets faint. Through impatience, unbelief, and wilfulness; through indolence, and sloth, and coldness; through neglect of prayer, and self-denial, and holy endurance—the Christ-derived life within us may seem almost ready to die. "But, if we hold ourselves still upon God; hold on by the thought that, as the new wine is in the cluster, there is in us a Divinity, an inspiration, a vital spark, put there by the Lord from heaven, our hopes will soon revive. The presence of Christ is with us, and our safety is to abide under its shadow. 'With Thee is the fountain of life,' says the Psalmist. All reviving influences come from that spring—to strengthen, to heal, to assuage, to satisfy."

And, brethren, not only does Christ give to us spiritual life here, but by His resurrection He has given to us a pledge and assurance of living hereafter. "Because He lives, we shall live also." There are some who believe in the doctrine of conditional immortality. They think that no one but those who sleep in Jesus shall be raised again from the dead. Now we do not dare to speculate about the fate of those who are not in Christ; but we are taught by God's word to believe that those who are in Jesus Christ are children of the resurrection, and heirs through Him of eternal life. "My sheep," He says, "hear My voice, and I know them, and they follow Me. And I give unto them eternal life; and they shall never perish, neither shall any man pluck them out of My hand."

XXVII.

WORLDLINESS.

"If any man love the world, the love of the Father is not in him."—1 JOHN ii. 15.

HERE the love of God and the love of the world are pronounced to be incompatible, just as our Lord said, "Ye cannot serve God and Mammon." We shall therefore discover what worldliness is, and what there is in the world which ought to be shunned, if we try to realize to ourselves what is meant by loving God. If God is the name for all that is good, true, and holy, raised to the infinite and represented in a person, to love Him must mean to love these attributes. No man, however, can know the Father except through the Son, by whom His character has been revealed. St. John's principle, then, will enable us to define worldliness as being all that prevents us from loving Christ. Those are unworldly who love Him and try to follow in His footsteps; those are worldly who, though they may say "Lord, Lord!" take not up their cross and follow Him.

Are we to withdraw ourselves from the legitimate business and recreation of the world? Certainly not, but only from the sins connected with them. Indeed, we cannot be said to be unworldly unless we live in the world and yet be not of the world. He is the Christ-like man who goes through the world's business and pleasures and yet remains unworldly still. Christ never shunned the world, for He did not come to call the righteous, but sinners to repentance. His mission led Him to the marriage feast and the publican's dinner. He would not have it thought that gloom, melancholy, and weariness formed a necessary part of His religion. His disciples were not told to cultivate morbid sadness for His sake, nor to be angry with themselves if nature assert her rights and animal spirits proclaim the world to be very fair. He said that they could not be sad so long as the Bridegroom was with them. He knew, of course, that all who hunger and thirst after righteousness must feel a Divine discontent with themselves; but He would not have them sorrow as those who have no hope, for "they shall be filled." Christ's followers are not to deny themselves legitimate pleasures, merely because they are pleasures, nor to think that their Father in heaven is pleased with their sorrows, as Baal's worshippers did when they cut themselves with knives and lances. Sacrifice He taught, but never sacrifice for its own sake; always for a worthy object—for the kingdom of heaven, for truth, for honour, for love.

But if worldliness does not consist in associating with our fellow sinners, being happy, and enjoying innocent pleasures, still less does it in loving the men and women that are in the world. We cannot love God, whom we have not seen, if we do not love our brother, whom we have seen. If we try to love God more by loving our friends less, we shall most likely, in the end, cease to love anything else but ourselves. Nor does worldliness consist in busying ourselves with our professions and employments; for these are forms of work, and all work is sanctified when done in Christ's spirit. All depends upon the spirit in which we work. A barrister, for instance, is worldly if his only thought is to put money in his purse; but surely by profession he is on the side of right, and may follow Christ by trying to support justice and truth. The profession of a merchant is good in itself; and yet if he spend twelve hours daily in thinking of and working for money, how dwelleth the love of God in him? When the soldiers and publicans asked John the Baptist what they should do, he did not tell them to give up their professions, but only the vices connected with them. Work is part of religion, as, indeed, everything may be, if we obey St. Paul's command, "Whether, therefore, ye eat or drink, or whatsoever ye do, do all the glory of God." It is not unworldliness to live away from the world's occupations; but it is to live above them, each doing his work in an unworldly spirit. This is too often forgotten, and people talk of the world as something with which Christ's Church has no concern. As if our Master, by taking man's nature upon Him, had not commended to all His followers the noble maxim: "Nothing concerning man do I think indifferent to Me."

Having now tried to show that, in order to be unworldly, Christ's followers need not and should not separate themselves from the interests of the world, we must go on to inquire what worldliness really is, and when we should begin to suspect ourselves of it. "It is plain," says Bishop Butler, "that there is a capacity in the nature of man which neither riches, nor honours, nor sensual gratifications, nor anything in this world, can perfectly fill up or satisfy; there is a deeper and more essential want than any of these things can be the supply of." Now, I think worldly people are those who never truly seek after God, who alone could satisfy this capacity; those in whom this want has ceased to make itself felt amidst the selfishness of their everyday existence; those to whom pleasure, business, and themselves are a "supply," instead of love towards God and desire to benefit men; whose "being's end and aim" is to get honours and riches; who do not love all their fellow men because they are

Christ's brothers and because He died for them, but only those amongst them who have fine connections, numerous servants, a large house, or some such good things of this world to render them "worth knowing" and loving.

"Is it inconsistent with our loving God?"—this is the test by which worldliness is discovered. It is the practical atheism of living without God in the world. And this all do who do not aspire to be like Him, to bring their wills into conformity with His, and to love what He loves.

If while living in the world we would live above it, and save our souls from its petrifying influence, we must set our affections on things above, and not on the "fleeting show" of the world, which is not our home, but only a school, in which we are being trained for the inheritance which our Heavenly Father has in store for us. And surely no generation requires to be reminded of this more than our own, for—

> "The world is too much with us, late and soon
> Getting and spending, we lay waste our powers."

Like the Sadducees of old, we seem to believe neither in Angel nor Spirit, but only in "getting on" and being considered "respectable." No doubt if un-worldliness consisted in talking about God, there is enough of that; but it is to be feared that during six days of the week we, in this nineteenth century, really forget that a living God exists, and that it is according to His will, and not according to public opinion, that we should regulate our actions. If this be the case, it is no wonder that in our professions and business we work with eye-service as men-pleasers, instead of being the servants of Christ doing the will of God from the heart. But why should we not set our affections on the world? Is not its fruit good for food and pleasant to the eye? Because, in St. John's words, "If man love the world, the love of the Father is not in Him. And the world passeth away and the lust thereof; but he that doeth the will of God abideth for ever." The first reason, then, is because excessive love of the world is incompatible with love towards God. One of these two must be the object of our affections. No one is sufficient for himself. We must all have some external object round which our affections may centre. Even the most selfish soon discover that life would be unbearable if they ceased altogether to care for anything but for themselves. If, then, we try to satisfy the famine which is in our souls, when we have nothing to love, with the husks of the world, we shall be tempted to remain away from our Father's home; and thus contenting ourselves with loving the world, the love of the Father is not in us. But "whosover drinketh of this shall thirst again." Our nature is capable of infinite love, and if we try to satisfy it with nothing more than the finite, fleeting things of the world we must sooner or later discover the hollowness and unsatisfactoriness of all created things, and ask, in despair, "Who will show us any good?" And to this there is but one answer, that of the Psalmist: "Lord, lift Thou up the light of Thy countenance upon us!" The infinite perfection of our Heavenly Father can alone satisfy the souls of His children, who are made after His likeness. We cannot escape degradation, if, formed to love God, we make terms with the world; if instead of preserving untarnished those ideals of holiness and goodness which we find in us, and which should tell us that we are not of the earth earthy, but the children of Him from whom they spring, we content ourselves with conventional respectability, consider this life perfect if it would only last, and cease to long for a better. Far lower than the brutes may man sink if, made in God's image, he never place before himself even an ideal of goodness, nor approve of anything more excellent than what he can find in the world. The second reason why we should not too much love the world, is because both it and the "lust thereof" passeth away. The transitoriness of the world is twofold. First, the things in it soon pass, as a tale that is told; secondly, we soon lose our desire and capacity of enjoying them—"the lust thereof." As to the transitory nature of the things of the world, it is evident enough. Change is stamped on every thing. Empires, creeds, and nations disappear, and others fill their place. Even the particles which compose our bodies are renewed every seven years. But even if all that is in the world did not thus pass away, the lust of the eye, and the pride of life soon do. We cannot long enjoy; and the greater the pleasure is, the sooner it will cease. When we become men we put away childish things. In middle age we cannot cloy the hungry edge of pampered appetite with the pleasures which satisfied our youth. The old, too, have to confess—

> "But yet I know where'er I go
> That there hath passed away a glory from the earth."

The more we enjoy the less we are capable of enjoying, though it does not become easier, but much more difficult, to live without our tasteless pleasures. How few, after a short time, really enjoy the so-called pleasures in which they engage! We cheat ourselves into thinking that we are happy when doing what other pleasure-seekers do. We imagine that we are enjoying the things we think we ought to enjoy, and cling to them from habit, when our hearts are far from them. And thus we go on cheating ourselves and shirk the question, "Wherefore do ye spend money for that which is not bread, and your labour for that which satisfieth not?" But all are agreed on this subject of the shortness of life and the fleeting, hollow nature of its pleasures; though the conclusion of their whole matter may not be as wise as Solomon's: "Fear God and keep His commandments." Still, all who have, like him, given their hearts to know wisdom and to know madness and folly, and to prove them with mirth, and who have seen all the works that are done under the sun, echo the royal preacher's sad experience: "Vanity of vanities, all is vanity." In this, at least, poets, *blasé* men of fashion, and sentimentalists, agree with the Christian. Yet they make a very different use of their knowledge. The sentimentalist bids us not to love the world; but since he does not substitute anything for it, he only increases our misery, for he takes our little all and leaves us nothing. The man of pleasure says, "Let us eat and drink, for to-morrow we die"; and if we to follow his example we shall die, for "he that soweth to the flesh shall of the flesh reap corruption." With far different thoughts, however, does the true Christian contemplate the change and decay that are on all the things he sees. He is not without hope, because he does not live without God in the world. He knows that whatever else may pass away, what he does for His Master cannot. The effect of his action may not be great, and he may from ignorance have left undone things which he ought to have done, and done things which he ought not to have done; but throughout eternity and amidst the crash of worlds nothing can destroy the love which gives even a cup of cold water in Christ's name and for His sake.

XXVIII.

BID CHRIST TO YOUR WEDDING.

"And both Jesus was called, and His disciples, to the marriage."—JOHN ii. 2.

WOULD to God that His dear Son were bidden to all weddings as to that of Cana! Truly then the wine of consolation and blessing would never be lacking. He who desires that the young of his flock should be like Jacob's, fair and ring-straked, must set fair objects before their eyes; and he who would find a blessing in his marriage must ponder the holiness aud dignity of this mystery, instead of which too often weddings become a season of mere feasting and disorder.

A new home is being formed, in reference to which the bride and bridegroom should think: "This is none other but the house of God, and this is the gate of heaven. As for me and my house, we will serve the Lord."

A church or chapel is called "God's house," but if every one rightly used matrimony, every house in the parish might be called the same.

Home is the place of the highest joy; religion should sanctify it. Home is the sphere of the deepest sorrows; the highest consolation of religion should assuage its griefs. Home is the place of the greatest intimacy of heart with heart; religion should sweeten it with the joy of confidence. Home discovers all faults; religion should bless it with the abundance of charity. Home is the place for impressions, for instruction and culture; there should religion open her treasures of wisdom and pronounce her heavenly benediction.

An old minister, previous to the meeting of the General Assembly of the Church of Scotland, used to pray that the assembly might be so guided as "no' to do ony harm." We have often thought that such a prayer as this would be an appropriate commencement for the marriage service. Considering the issues that are involved in marriage—the misery unto the third and fourth generation that may result from it—those who join together man and woman in matrimony ought to pray that in doing so they may do no harm.

In a form of marriage ceremony which is largely recognized by the Society of Friends, the bridegroom says, "I promise, in the fear of the Lord, to love, cherish," &c. People are happy in married life only when in this spirit they take and keep their marriage vows.

It would not be kind to advise a young pair who have leaped into the dark of married life not to think of God. He is a Saviour from trouble rather than a troubler, and the husband and wife who never try to serve Him will not be likely to serve each other, or to gain much real happiness from their marriage.

There are many foolish and ignorant sayings connected with the rite of marriage. One of these is: "Happy is the bride the sun shines on." It would be far more true to say, "Happy is the bride God shines on." Ask His blessing, and, in spite of passing showers, either of rain or of troubles, all will be well.

The following is related of the well-known Mary Somerville: When a girl, she and her brother had coaxed their timid mother to accompany them for a sail. The day was sunny, but a stiff breeze was blowing, and presently the boat began to toss and roll. "George," Mrs. Fairfax called, to the man in charge, "this is an awful storm! I fear we are in great danger; mind how you steer: remember I trust in you!" "Dinna trust in me, leddy; trust in God Almighty." In terror the lady exclaimed, "Dear me, is it come to that!" To that it ought to come on the day of marriage quite as much as on the day of death. It is not only in times of danger and distress that we want God's presence, but in the time of our well-being, when all goes merry as a marriage-bell. Live away from Him, and the happiness you enjoy to-day may become your misery to-morrow.

Young married people are surprised when they discover that the honeymoon is not entirely composed of honey. Even the first year of married life is not always the happiest, thought it ought always to be very happy. Living together happily is an art which the most affectionate couple cannot ordinarily learn in a year. Each has to make some unpleasant discoveries and to overcome some fixed inclinations. True happiness begins when these discoveries have been made, and each is thoroughly resolved to make the other as happy as possible for all time.

After the honeymoon, husband and wife too often renounce not merely those pretty arts to please which belonged to the time of wooing, but even common politeness towards each other. And yet Christian courtesy, like charity, should begin at home.

The honeymoon is over, and the young couple have exchanged their chrysalis condition for the pleasures and duties of ordinary married life. Let them begin by forming a very high ideal of marriage. Now and on every anniversary of their wedding-day they should seriously reflect on those vows, which are too often taken either in entire ignorance of their meaning and import, or thoughtlessly, as though they were mere incidents of the marriage ceremony.

Those who have read my book, "How to be Happy though Married," know how important I consider it to be that people should learn the duties and responsibilities of marriage before undertaking them. This book is now in the eighth edition, and has been translated into French, German, and Dutch, a fact which shows that there are not a few who desire to read anything that they think may possibly enable them to know and do matrimonial duties. Believe me, brethren, this knowledge and power come from no book, but only from the Spirit of Christ speaking to your hearts: therefore bid Him to your wedding.

XXIX.

OLD TESTAMENT HEROES.

"Gideon, Barak, Samson, Jephthah, David, Samuel, and the prophets ... of whom the world was not worthy."—HEBREWS xi. 32, 38.

IN estimating the characters recorded of Old Testament heroes, people often fall into two opposite errors. One is, the error of those who fancy that when any one is praised in the Bible, every act of his life is approved of by God and held up to us as an example; the other error is, to insist on testing the characters of such men as Gideon, Barak, Samson, and David by the nineteenth-century standard of morality, and if they appear—as they must—to be often cruel, treacherous, and in many things below that standard, to make no allowance for the time, place, and circumstances in which their lives were cast. To both these classes of incapable judges we may say, as Balak did to Balaam, "Neither curse them at all, nor bless them at all." We have said that some persons hold the mistaken opinion that in the Bible every action of such men's lives is praised, which is certainly not the case. They think that it would be profane to criticise freely the characters of men who received from God the sentence of approval, "Well done, good and faithful servant," though this was given not surely because they never were cruel, never were deceitful, never were guilty of any sin, but because they resolutely, manfully, and in spite of all obstacles, performed the task which God had given them to do. It was "through faith" that they "obtained a good report." That is to say, they believed in God's ever-present, governing power more than those did amongst whom they lived. They believed also that they, themselves, were workers together with Him, and they did His work in rough, stormy times with a heart and a will. Whatever God found for their hands to do, they did it with all their might.

Do not let us call evil good, and distort our consciences so far as to say that every action in the lives of such men as Samson and David was perfectly good. This the Bible does not say, but even if it did, we must not turn a deaf ear to our consciences when they speak to us of anything, even of the Bible itself. Indeed, to do so would destroy our proof that the Bible is *the* book of all others which is most inspired by God. For how could we know at all that the Bible is the word of God if it did not prove itself to our consciences to be such? All good books, no doubt, are inspired by God, for "every good and every perfect gift is from above, and cometh down from the Father of lights," but none so much as the Bible, and it is our conscience which tells us that this is the case. Conscience is the only ultimate guide God has given us to His truth. As the eye gives light to the body, so does conscience to the soul. If the light, then, that is in us be darkness, how great is that darkness! And we may be sure that this light will be darkness if we put it not in a candlestick, but under the bushel of an infallible book, an infallible Pope, an infallible party watchword, or anything else. Let us not, through false modesty, silence our conscience, or substitute anything in its place, for it is the voice of God speaking to us, and we must take heed lest, peradventure, we be found even to fight against God. No Bible could be true which contradicted a good man's conscience, nor could an interpretation of any part of that Bible be the right one from which his moral nature recoiled. Let us listen to that safe guide, Bishop Butler. After pointing out that "objections against Christianity itself are in a great measure frivolous," because, "upon supposition of a revelation, it is highly credible beforehand we should be incompetent judges of it to a certain degree," he goes on to say, "I express myself with caution, lest I should be mistaken to vilify reason; which is, indeed, the only faculty wherewith to judge concerning anything, even revelation itself: or be misunderstood to assert, that a supposed revelation cannot be proved false, from internal characters. For, it may contain clear immoralities or contradictions; and either of these would prove it false."[1] The second class of persons we spoke of are therefore right in criticising Bible characters by the light of their consciences which the Father of Lights has given to them; but they are wrong in not taking into consideration the barbarous age in which these men lived, and the cruel God-less world around, which was not worthy of them.

To judge fairly of any man we must, by an effort of imagination, put ourselves in the circumstances of his case, consider what his education and parentage were, and try to feel the strength of the temptations to which he was subjected. This requires more thought, sympathy, and imagination than many of us are capable of, so that we should be very careful how we judge any man. Let us hope that most of the hard judgments we hear pronounced are suggested by this want of thought and imagination, rather than from a want of kindness and Christian charity.

The Bible is a history, or kind of school report, of the education with which God has been training the human race. The human race has had an infancy, boyhood, and middle-age, as individuals have had. When it was a child, it spake as a child, it understood as a child, it thought as a child; but when it

[1] "Analogy," Part II. Chap. III.

became a man, it put away childish things. As education is revelation coming to the individual man, so revelation is education which has come and is coming to the human race. And just as a wise teacher does not reveal all the culture and knowledge of his mind to an infant, but only as much as it is able to bear, so God did not reveal His law and character all at once, but "line upon line, precept upon precept, here a little, and there a little," just as mankind could understand and appreciate them. We are not, therefore, to expect to find as high moral teaching and as true conceptions of God's character in the mouths of the patriarchs, who represented the babes of the human race, as we learn from God's holy prophets. Then, again, it required the fulness of Him that filleth all things, even the light of the Sun of Righteousness, to complete and explain prophetical teaching. Our Lord says that Moses gave his precepts, not because they were the best possible, but because the hardness of his people's hearts prevented them from receiving better. The law was by no means perfect. There were many cruel and unjust precepts in it, as we see, now that our eyes have been enlightened by the Spirit of Christ, and by such teaching as the Sermon on the Mount. The law was our "schoolmaster to bring us to Christ;" the true meaning of which expression is, that the law was the servant, or attendant, who brought us to the school of Christ. Thus, the whole of Scripture history teaches us the truth, which we are generally too slow in acknowledging, that—

> "Our little systems have their day,
>   They have their day and cease to be;
>   They are but broken lights of Thee,
>   And Thou, O Lord, art more than they."

We ought not, then, to judge of Gideon, Barak, Samson, and David by the higher standard of morality which God has given to us. Let us look to their example as of men who were not without faults, but who nevertheless tried to live above their world; who endeavoured to battle for God and His right, instead of taking up with the prevalent unbelief and abominable wickedness of the world in the midst of which they lived, and which was not worthy of them. And surely as such they are lights shining in a dark place to us, as they were to their contemporaries. We, too, however clearer our light may be than theirs was, may receive strength from their example to be very courageous for God in the midst of a crooked and perverse generation. They were more believing and better than their world, though perhaps more cruel and barbarous than the generality of Christians. They fought the Lord's battle against all who hated Him. Are we, with all our boasted "Christian experiences," above our world now as they were above theirs then, or only on a level with it? Do we try to fight God's battle against the dishonest maxims which a money-loving generation has introduced into business of all kinds? Do we maintain His truth as He has revealed it to us in opposition to popular lies? Do we try to win over all gainsayers, by representing the religion of Christ not as a collection of lifeless dogmas, or as a sickly sentiment and unnatural system of restraint upon the innocent recreations of life, but rather a cheerful, manly life lived in Christ's strength? In social intercourse do we try to raise the sentiment and conversation of those with whom we meet, instead of sinking to the conventional watermark? Have we courage to obey God's commands as these men had of whom it is said that "they were stoned, they were sawn asunder, were tempted, were slain with the sword; they wandered about in sheepskins and goatskins; being destitute, afflicted, tormented?" Are we not often cowardly in the sight of men, though far too fearless in the sight of God? Do not many, for instance, run into debt because they fear to appear poor in the sight of men, and desire to get credit by false appearances for riches which they do not possess? That is to say, they wish to appear rich in the sight of men, though by their dishonesty they well know that they must appear very poor in the sight of God. Do we try to avoid unjust anger, lies, discontent, and all those sins which are hardly considered to be sins at all because every one commits them, but which we must try to avoid before we dare profess to be living above our world as these heroes did above theirs?

As long as we are conformed to the "lust of the flesh, the lust of the eye, and the pride of life, which is not of the Father but of the world;"—as long as we are satisfied with fixing on individual men in order to stigmatize them as "the world," saying, "We are Christians, ye are of the world," while we do not ourselves try to overcome that wordly spirit which in some of its infinitely various manifestations has a swept and garnished home in the hearts of most of us;—as long as we are satisfied with the low standard of goodness which most of us have—in all these ways we are fighting on the side of the world against God. With all our civilization, education, and the glorious light of the Gospel of Christ shining on us, Gideon, Barak, Samson, and David shall rise in judgment against us. For these men of God lived above their world, which was not worthy of them; while we live on a level with ours, which is quite worthy of us, for we are in everything conformed to it.

Thus it is that the noble army of martyrs and goodly fellowship of God's servants that have served their generation and are fallen asleep, are living at this hour; that they are with us as witnesses of our acts and failures: to reprove us if we are selfish men: to encourage us to walk in cheerful godliness: and to show us how, by loving and fearing God, we may escape from the popular evils of our time, and need not fear what man can do unto us.

XXX.

ARE CHRISTIAN PRINCIPLES PRACTICAL?

"But I say unto you, That ye resist not evil; but whosoever shall smite thee on thy right cheek, turn to him the other also. Give to him that asketh thee, and from him that would borrow of thee turn not thou away. Therefore I say unto you, Take no thought [Be not anxious, R.V.] for your life, what ye shall eat, or what ye shall drink; nor yet for your body, what ye shall put on."—MATTHEW v. 39, 42; vi. 25.

THESE and other similar commands present great difficulties to many sincere Christians. They find that it is impossible to obey them literally unless they act as madmen and oppose the whole of the world's legitimate every-day proceedings. Yet they have an uncomfortable feeling that perhaps they are inconsistent for not doing so, or come to the no less erroneous conclusion that a Christian life cannot be realized in modern society—that it can only be lived out by abandoning the world and its concerns, and that, therefore, a practical man who has to earn his bread and support his family cannot follow Christ.

Is it then possible, or even right, to literally obey the precepts in these and other verses concerning non-resistance to violence, almsgiving and providence, or forethought? Certainly there is no question which is answered—when it is not shirked *altogether* — with less straightforwardness and sincerity than this. We preach and profess what we never dream of practising, and what we could not practise so long as the social state and laws of Europe continue as they are. It may therefore be useful to try and point out how, in these cases, as in so many others, it is the letter that killeth, and the spirit that giveth life. How such precepts of Christ are "a guide to the spirit we must cherish, not to the conduct we must pursue." How, lastly, it would be impossible to obey literally such particular precepts without disobeying the very principles which suggested them, and opposing the whole spirit of our Lord's teaching. Now the first precept—" But I say unto you, That ye resist not evil; but whosoever shall smite thee on thy right cheek, turn to him the other also "—never has been literally obeyed by any body of Christians. For even those who did not resist evil, never went the length of facilitating attack. No sane Christian ever turned his left cheek to him who smote him on the right. Because our laws are well administered, it is seldom now that blows are aimed at us, and when they are, the necessity for self-defence and resistance to evil is taken out of our hands. We pay taxes and employ the police to resist for us. So long as bad people exist in the world, if they are not to get the upper hand, there must be police and laws to restrain and punish them. Who among us would advocate their abolition? Yet so long as police and laws resist evil for us, this precept of non-resistance, which we are now considering, is not obeyed in the letter, though in spirit it may be. Nor can it be considered brotherly love not to resist the violent. For the worst ill service you can do them is to allow them to go unpunished. By doing so you encourage them in their violence, and make them heap up wrath against the day of wrath. It is not humane towards themselves, and very cruel towards the gentle and good, who would soon be trampled under by the brutal and bad if these were permitted to become "masters of the situation." Thus it is that the Spirit of Christ, or brotherly love, demands that on some occasions we should resist evil. What, then, can we learn from this command if it cannot, and should not, be obeyed literally? Is it not " to cultivate the temper which will effectually prevent us from being quick to resent, prone to retaliate, or severe to punish," but in such a way as not to contradict the natural instincts which God has given us, or the spirit of our Lord's teaching?

We now consider the precept—"Give to him that asketh thee, and from him that would borrow of thee turn not thou away." Would it be beneficial to society to literally obey this precept? or is it not true that if you were to give to every one that asked you, idleness and drunkenness would be greatly encouraged, and much harm done to society? Surely no conclusion is better established than that all indiscriminate almsgiving not only does injury to the objects of it, in whom it fosters all mean and unChristian vices, but to the deserving poor, from whom it diverts sympathy. Indeed, it is not too much to say that indiscriminate almsgiving is a sentimental self-indulgence, which every thoughtful Christian should resist. How, then, are we to interpret the precept—" Give to him that asketh thee?" We are first to reflect that the Gospel was not meant to supply a code of rules which would pass away with circumstances, but general principles which should guide the action of every age and every condition of society; that we are to acquire the same mind that was in Christ, and to let our behaviour flow freely from that. After making due allowance for the Eastern manner of speaking, perhaps the reason why our Lord clothed His teaching in an exaggerated, paradoxical form was, that he wished to prevent those attempts at obeying the letter and neglecting the spirit which had corrupted and killed all spiritual life in the religious world of His day. Christ desired us to do all the good we can to our fellow-creatures, especially to the poor and helpless. He would have us to elevate, not to degrade them; to foster their Christian virtues, not their selfish vices; and the very texts that we read as enjoining almsgiving are just those which, rightly interpreted, in the present state of society distinctly prohibit it. What we have to ask ourselves is, " What would Christ, with all the circumstances before Him, have directed in these times?" We see then what is the true use of Scripture. That it is a direct guide only so far forth as we are circumstanced exactly like the persons to whom it was originally addressed. We are to ask ourselves, If so-and-so was the duty of men in such circumstances, what is our duty when we are thus otherwise circumstanced? And it will often happen, when all the circumstances are totally different, that in order to obey the spirit we shall be obliged to disregard the letter.

We consider, lastly, the precept—"Take no thought for the morrow." At the time when the Bible was translated, the phrase "take thought" meant to distress or trouble oneself. To "die of thought," in old English meant to die of a broken heart. We find "take thought" used in this sense in 1 Samuel ix. 5, where Saul says to his servant, "Come and let us return, lest my father leave caring for the asses and take thought for us." There is, therefore, no difficulty in the precept—"Take no thought for the morrow," for it means take no over-anxious self-disturbing thought. But even suppose the English phrase had not thus changed its meaning, this precept would present no difficulty to those who seek for the spirit of their Master's teaching below the letter or envelope in which it has been conveyed to them. Consider, first, how impossible it is that our Lord should have desired us to take no care at all for the morrow. For is it not certain that the man who, out of a good income or good wages, fails to lay up for a rainy day, and takes no care to make provision for his family, is guilty of a great sin? St. Paul tells every man to "labour, working with his hands the thing which is good"—not certainly to satisfy selfish greediness, but "that he may have to give to him that needeth." And he goes so far as to say that "if any provide not for his own, and especially for those of his own house, he hath denied the faith, and is worse than an infidel." Indeed, if our working-classes are ever to emerge from their present most unsatisfactory condition; if they are to become respectable citizens and true Christians, they must learn, where they can, to save for to-morrow's needs. How then are we to reconcile this duty of providing for the future with the precept—"Take no thought for the morrow?" By considering that these words of Christ only concern that one side of truth on which at the moment His thoughts were fixed. He was bidding His hearers not to be weighed down with those worldly cares which, if too anxiously attended to, would undo all His teaching. Now we have no right to use a precept addressed to those among whom this anxious carefulness for the future was in excess, to excuse our deficiency in the virtue of prudence. Had Jesus preached to Englishmen of the middle and lower classes, we may feel certain He would have used very different language. Is it not probable that He would have reproved their improvident habits in some such words as these—"Take thought for to-morrow, and provide for its necessities, in order that when to-morrow comes you may be free enough from sordid wants and gnawing cares to have some moments to spare for the things which belong unto your peace?"

This, then, appears to be the true way for Christians of our day to deal with such questions as those we have been considering, and such other ones as the sharing of property, which last we find, from the Acts of the Apostles, was a practice of the early Christians. "Neither said any of them that ought of the things which he possessed was his own, but they had all things in common." From which verse we should learn — while recognizing all the benefits which society derives from the institution of private property—to consider all our possessions and talents as held in trust, and only lent to us by God in order that with them we may benefit others. The Christian law is the spirit of Christ, which is the source from which all right action flows. Therefore we can and ought to obey the Christian rule of life even in our present very complicated state of society, though in order to do so we must penetrate by careful thought to the true spirit and meaning of Christ's teaching. Let us not forget that Christianity is not a set of precepts, but a life—the life of Christ lived not away from the world, but amidst its scenes of business and lawful pleasures. Now this life may be lived in every age, and under all sorts of conditions. We have heard a clergyman say that a man once told him, when he objected to something in his dealings as being dishonest, "That may be religion, sir, but you see it is not in the way of business." Now surely if Christianity is not "in the way of business"—if it does not influence our daily life and make us better men, it is of very little use to us. Its teaching is vain if it leave us in our sins, or is only a Sunday matter to be put off with our best clothes before going to our Monday's business.

Christ now appears to all who, by God's help, will not go away, in an age when many are forsaking Him, to prove that His religion is a thoroughly real thing and of practical use, by showing themselves "patterns of good works"—by adorning the doctrine of God our Saviour in all things. And certainly if the religion of Jesus makes those who profess it more honest and God-fearing than those who do not; if it make them more truthful, loving, and gentle; if it save them from the secret faults which can only be known to God and their own souls—then it cannot be said by the greatest sceptic that it is a vain thing for them because it is their life. Oh, may we not be found ready to give Him a Judas kiss of recognition when amongst religious people on Sunday, and then just as ready to betray Him by our week-day thoughts, words, and actions!

XXXI.

CHRISTIAN SOCIALISM.

"And one of the company said unto Him, Master, speak to my brother, that he divide the inheritance with me. And He said unto him, Man, who made Me a judge or a divider over you? And He said unto them, Take heed and beware of covetousness."—LUKE xii. 13-15.

THERE is no doubt that the greatest question of the day in Europe and even in America is Socialism. What do we mean by the term? According to my dictionary, Socialism is "the science which has for its object the improvement of social arrangements." With such a science as this it is obvious that every Christian ought to sympathize. What he cannot always sympathize with, is the means that are suggested or used for the improvement of these social arrangements. He may think that the remedy is worse than the disease, or that more injury upon the whole would result from its adoption. Socialism ought to be carefully distinguished from Communism; but the two words are often indiscriminately used, and this confusion renders Socialism odious to many, for—

> "What is a Communist? One who hath yearnings,
> For equal divisions of unequal earnings.
> Idler or bungler, or both, he is willing
> To fork out his penny and pocket your shilling."

"The magic of property," says Arthur Young, "turns sand into gold." It has done more in this country to produce a spirit of self-help than State aid for the whole planet ever could do. Communists speak of property as robbery and sin, but it the very heart of social progress, and every one who studies the interests of mankind will do his best to defend that heart from being split open by the communistic dagger. The Church, in all her branches, while inculcating philanthropy, insists with St. Paul on self-help. "If any would not work, neither should he eat." The Thessalonians were told to "work with their own hands." Indeed, the Apostle goes so far as to say that if "any provide not for his own, and especially for those of his own house, he hath denied the faith, and is worse than an infidel." In thus teaching the duty and necessity of self-help, the Church proves herself to be the chief friend of the poor. Not so Communism. By destroying the right of personal ownership in the means of production, and by fostering dependence on State-help, it undermines the energy and self-help of all classes, and is the enemy of the poor quite as much as of the rich.

But was there not, many ask, a community of goods, and were not all things in common, in the primitive Church at Jerusalem. Certainly, but this community of goods was not compulsory, but purely voluntary. It did not come about by any sort of confiscation. "While it remained, was it not thine own?" were the words addressed to Ananias; "and after it was sold, was it not in thine own power?" It was a voluntary act of love rather than a duty. Still less was it a right which the majority might assert against individuals. There was no community of goods absolutely and universally enforced by apostolic precept, or as a necessary and permanent arrangement of the Church. This is plain from the scope of the almsdeeds of Dorcas; from Mary the mother of Mark retaining her house; from Mnason's ability to provide lodgings; from the Hebrew Christians having property of which they could be despoiled; from the exhortations to almsgiving and to the distinct duties of rich and poor in the Epistles generally; and from the recommendation to the Corinthians in particular that every one should lay by on the first day of the week as God had prospered him. The estimate of comparative needs recognized when these Jerusalem Christians parted their possessions to all men, as every man had need, shows clearly that property was not alienated beyond control.

This, then, was very different from the Communism taught at the present day, which demands an equality enforced by a central authority, and which, so far from inculcating a spirit of self-denial, looks for the self-indulgence of all.

Mordern Communists affirm that Communism was the natural outcome of the Liberty, Equality, and Fraternity implied in Christ's teaching. That the principle did not hold its ground is ascribed by them to the ambition and worldliness of the Church as she increased in power, especially after her official recognition as the State religion of the Roman Empire. After this alliance with wealth and grandeur, they say the Church rapidly departed from the simplicity of the Gospel, and consoled herself by the acquisition of temporal aggrandisement for her disappointment in not attaining to the long-deferred hope of a final "restitution of all things."

On the other hand, the defenders of the principle of individual property as opposed to Communism (which in their opinion is a "mutiny against society") deny that the Church ever sanctioned officially, or that her Founder ever recommended, such a custom as that of " having all things in common."

As a matter of fact, we may say with an able Church historian, that the community in Jerusalem growing out of the society of the apostles, who were accustomed already to the common purse system, hit upon the daring plan of establishing a community of goods. And this was fostered by the first outburst of enthusiastic brotherly love, being all the more readily accepted in consequence of the prevailing expectation among the disciples of the approaching subversion of all things.

According to this explanation, the Communism practised by the early Church was not so much a rigid logical deduction from the teaching of Christ as it was the result of spontaneous "Love of the Brethren," who were all united by the same common bond, and all equally ready to devote their goods and possessions to the common welfare.

One great idea was ever before the minds of this small band of early Christians, that the great coming catastrophe, "the end of all things," was at hand. Property and position, and indeed all worldly matters, were consequently regarded by them as of secondary importance on the eve of such a momentous crisis.

Nowhere out of Jerusalem do we find any other early Christian community of goods. The arrangement at Jerusalem was not intended to be permanent, and perhaps those political economists are not far wrong who assert that it did more harm than good, and produced the chronic state of poverty that existed among "the poor saints at Jerusalem."

The Master Himself had left no definite instructions as to the future social organization of His "little flock." It had been His plan all along to lay down general principles, leaving them to be worked out in the course of time, rather than to prescribe definite lines of conduct under given circumstances. The ideal of a perfect society was ever held up by Him to His most intimate disciples. He formed no plan, however, for realizing this ideal in a political polity. The working out of His principles was left to the "new leaven" which was to reform character, and thus indirectly society. Our Lord always refused—as when the brother asked Him to become a divider of inheritance—to interfere with the outward circumstances of life as regards either government or finance. His kingdom does not depend on institutions, because it is to be established within the hearts of His subjects. It is the reign of God in man, and as such it is spiritual and invisible. Certainly the "sacredness of the money-bags," as it has been sneeringly called, is not upheld in the Gospel. On the contrary, wealth and pomp are regarded with contempt as compared with "the pearl of great price." The rich are taught to consider all their possessions as held in trust, and only lent to them by God for the service of the community as a whole. They are bound to be on their guard against doing harm with their riches—against demoralizing the poorer classes by profligate expenditure, by niggardliness, or, on the other hand, by careless almsgiving, by the temptations of their domestic service. Nor is it enough for them to cease to do evil with their money; they must learn to do good. And as for the pride of money, it should never be found amongst Christians, for our Lord laid down emphatically that in His kingdom men were to be esteemed worthy not in proportion to their wealth or hereditary rank, but in proportion to their capacity to serve. " Whosoever will be great among you, let him be your minister." Those whom the Gospel would have humble and meek are the rich, and great, and strong. The strong are to bear the infirmities of the weak, and the meek are to inherit the earth. " All of you be subject one to another."

> " Oh ! let us keep our proper stations,
> Bless the squire and his relations ;
> Be thankful for our daily rations,
> And humbly fill our occupations ! "

The duty of striving after such a standard of perfection as this has been preached rather more than enough to the poor, but the Bible tells the rich that they, too, have occupations, and that they must humbly fulfil them. The "patrimony of the poor" is not to be restored by means of violent social changes, but by moral influences working upon rich and poor alike. Christ's sympathy was with *all* classes, and He applied remedies to individuals in preference to propounding revolutionary theories for the construction of society.

But although the first heroic effort of the early Christian Socialists proved vain, the idea of a thorough social reformation in the Church, and by the Church, was not lost sight of, but has been cherished ever since by devout and noble souls at different periods of Church history. We have glimpses of it in the early Fathers; and it has found expression in the constitution of the monastic orders of the middle ages. It was again revived during the stormy periods of the Reformation and the Revolution, and is being carried into effect at this very moment, in a modified form, by the Moravians, and almost literally among some communistic religious societies in America.

The noble idea underlying these systems of Christian Socialism is the "great secret" of Christ's religion, the unpalatable doctrine of unselfishness and self-sacrifice; or, in modern phraseology, it is the doctrine of *Altruism* as opposed to *Egoism*; in a higher sense, the principle of Christian Socialism as opposed to un-Christian Individualism—not the Socialism of the Socialists, but the social theory formulated by St. Paul in his Epistle to the Philippians: "Look not every man on his own things, but every man also on the things of others. Let this mind be in you, which was also in Christ Jesus." The principle still remains in force that all our possessions, as well as all our gifts, although our own are to be held in trust for the general good of all— a principle essentially and distinctively Christian.

Happily the rich are beginning to recognize this truth. There is obviously an immense outgrowth in the generous distribution of wealth. But the rich have difficulties as well as the poor, and one of these lies in determining how to expend their money in a way that will prove beneficial to society. The question, "To whom or to what cause shall I contribute money?" must be a very anxious one to conscientious men of wealth. "How are we to measure," we may suppose rich men to ask, "the relative utility of charities? And then political economists are down upon us if by mistake we help those who might have helped themselves. It is easy to talk against our extravagance; tell us rather how to spend our money as becomes Christians;" that is to say for the greatest good of the greatest number. The fact is, riches must now be considered by all good men as a distinct profession, with responsibilities no less onerous than those of other professions. And this very difficult profession of wealth ought to be learned by studying social science and otherwise with as much care as the professions of divinity, law, and medicine are learned. When in this way the rich accept and prepare themselves for the duties of their high calling, it will cease to be a cause of complaint that in the nature of things money tends continually to fall into the hands of a few large capitalists.

The spirit of brotherly love which underlies Christian Socialism is being more and more understood in the present day. The great communistic principle, "All for each and each for all," is practically gaining ground. It is being applied in the case of all our philanthropic institutions, of our hospitals and benevolent societies, our voluntary schools and pious foundations, our free libraries and museums, our drinking fountains and public parks. Its spirit pervades our mild poor laws—mild to a fault; our laws for the protection of labour and for the provision of healthy homes for the industrial classes, our sanitary reforms, our private charities and systematic organization, and the numberless attempts to alleviate the misfortunes of the maimed, the halt and the blind, the wretched and the fallen; in fact, all efforts of the State and private individuals and associations to improve the condition of the less privileged members of society. These interferences of Government form practically a voluntary Communism, being an application of the funds of the wealthy for the benefit of the poor, a sort of sharing, so to speak, the "wealth of nations" among all, on the pattern of the early Christian Church.

But these interferences of Government must not be allowed to go too far. Self-help, not State-help, is the hope of the poor. Not State-help in the way of forced loans, providing dwellings for the poor and work for the unemployed, not the nationalization of land, not the abolition of inheritance; but the spirit of Christianity laying the foundation stone of self-help, and building up on it industry, honesty, foresight among the masses, until co-operative credit and co-operative production and industrial partnerships become possible and common—this is a slowly rising temple, of which the completion would be the joy of the whole earth.

XXXII.

SEEING NOT NECESSARILY BELIEVING.

"But I said unto you, That ye also have seen Me, and believe not."—JOHN vi. 36.

THERE is nothing which some people who are only half reasonable so much resent as being told that without faith they cannot be religious. They say or think somewhat in this way: "If religion be reasonable, where is the necessity for faith? if it be not, why should I believe in it? I believe what can be verified; with me, seeing is believing and nothing else."

Now it often happens that men see without believing, and believe in what they cannot see, so that seeing is not necessarily believing. Nothing is so deceptive as the senses. Every one knows what is meant by a "jaundiced view" of things; how the slightest change in the atmosphere, in diet, in exercise, renders us gay or sad, energetic or sluggish.

When Hamlet had lost his mirth " and foregone all custom of exercises," he says, " this goodly frame, the earth, seems to me a sterile promontory: this most excellent canopy, the air, look you—this brave o'erhanging—this majestical roof fretted with golden fire, why, it appears no other thing to me than a foul and pestilent congregation of vapours." Certainly a sceptic might easily persuade himself that there is nothing good or bad, great or small, happy or unhappy, but thinking makes it so. Nay, he might go further and say thinking itself is but " an idle waste of thought, and nought is everything and everything is nought," for our thoughts are coloured by our senses, and we have seen how little these are to be trusted when they are tossed to and fro and carried about by our sleight and cunning craftiness, whereby we lay in wait to deceive ourselves.

But even suppose our senses were trustworthy in giving us uniform perceptions, how are we to be sure that any external reality corresponds to our consciousness? You may see certain pictures on the back of your eye, but does it not require an act of faith to believe that these are anything more than subjective impressions ? If you take it as a fact that you see real objects, not merely images, you do it by a naked act of assumption, and possibly you may be imposing on yourself in so doing. Now if it be the case that faith is necessary even for such an ordinary operation as seeing, if without trust in some persons and some things we could not live at all in the world;

if physical philosophers, no less than other thinkers, must make some assumption, as, for instance, that the past uniform acting of nature's laws will continue to-morrow, why should faith be sneered at as if it were something invented by theologians to save themselves the trouble of thinking and answering awkward questions? If the commonest acts of intelligence are impossible without faith, it is strange that many who claim to be clever should despise it.

The Jews saw our Lord's miracles; but they did not believe them. They referred them to magic, or to the agency of evil spirits. We may be sure that if they could they would have denied them altogether; and their very efforts to explain phenomena to which they could not shut their eyes, in accordance with their theory that Jesus was not the Christ, is one of our strongest proofs that He was. We often fancy that if only we could see our Lord performing miracles, we should never be found faithless like the Jews. And yet the history of the Christian Church and of the regenerating power of the Gospel is much stronger evidence than any amount of startling wonders. Miracles performed before our eyes would greatly impress us, but this is very different from convincing us. We should believe such sights to be miracles, or account for them in commonplace ways, according as we were willing or unwilling to believe before seeing them. "But I say unto you," said our Lord Himself to the Jews, "that ye also have seen Me, and believe not."

The fact is, faith is ~~an act~~ *the will* *aims* of the mind and heart, not something forced upon us from without. As we cannot even believe that our senses testify truly to external realities without a certain venture of faith, so were God Himself to let us see His face, without dying, we should be impressed, but faithless still unless our minds and hearts exerted an act of faith. In order to believe at all, or indeed to reason, we must risk something in the way of an assumption. Seeing and believing, faith and demonstration—these must always be in their nature two different things. Those who demand for everything the evidence of their bodily senses, and only believe what they cannot help believing, simply refuse to *believe* anything, and demand to *know* everything.

Unfortunately there are a number of religious men, as well as scientific and literary, who persist in opposing faith to reason; though in the Bible it is always contrasted with sight, not with reason. Faith is the evidence of things not seen; but not of things unreasonable in the sense of contrary to reason. How much better friends are faith and science, culture and religion, than they think! We have endeavoured to remove the prejudice which considers faith as a sort of *Deus ex machina* for clearing up theological difficulties by pointing out how, without this despised faith, we could scarcely live at all, because we could trust nothing, not even our own senses.

To say of a religious doctrine, " Oh, I suppose I

must take it on faith," is no sneer, considering how many things we are forced to take upon faith in order to act at all, or even to live through a single day.

Our ideas and prejudices cling so much to words, that we must often change our words if we would preserve to things their true meaning. Were we to speak of "trust" rather than "faith," it would convey a much clearer meaning, and would at once connect faith with several kindred moral ideas, such as hope and love, more highly appreciated by untheological people. The Apostle who so often insisted on "justification by faith" seems, in one passage, to make hope synonymous with this faith, and he contrasts it with sight, as he does in the case of faith. "We are saved by hope; but hope that is seen is not hope; for what a man seeth why does he yet hope for?" Surely the experience of every one testifies in some measure to this saving power of hope or faith. If we despair of becoming better, we never shall become better. Sanguine men and nations do most and take the lead. We should better understand why it is that so much stress is laid on faith in the Bible, if we pictured to ourselves a monster who altogether disbelieved in any thing or person higher and better than himself, and even in his own better self. To see the purifying power of faith, we should imagine a man who wholly disbelieved in the possibility of goodness greater than his own; that is to say, who was a thorough atheist, who at the same time was so cynical as to doubt every man and woman, who, to complete his want of faith, doubted his own ideals, and all power to realize them. Should we not all say of such a one, "Let no such man be trusted?" What is it that makes men righteous, but trust or faith in the goodness of God, goodness of their fellow-creatures, and goodness in themselves; or rather, in power to attain to goodness? "I had fainted," says the Psalmist, "unless I had believed to see the goodness of the Lord in the land of the living." As regards faith in human nature, Dr. Arnold well remarked that *nil admirari* was the "Devil's motto." Every one remembers Shakspeare's words—

> "To thine own self be true,
> And it must follow, as the night the day,
> Thou can'st not be false to any man."

Surely those who depreciate faith must strangely misunderstand its nature.

It is a great pity that popular language should apply the same word faith to such distinct things as the faculty which apprehends unseen truths and the truths perceived by it. Much confusion would be avoided by distinguishing between that subjective faith which substantiates things unseen, and objective beliefs or creeds. As it is, we use the same words when we say that a man "has faith" in some person or principle, as when describing a creed we say, "this is the Catholic faith." We should call the spiritual faculty which discerns spiritual things "faith," and distinguish this from the intellectual frames, or creeds, in which the soul's discoveries are preserved.

Spiritual things are either spiritually discerned or not at all; but the setting or verbal statement which renders them fit for use and transmission, is the work of the intellect. Now it is this debating faculty or intellect which "ministers questions, rather than godly edifying, which is in faith."

The forms in which faith's discoveries are stated are never more than rough approximations to correctness, and have to be from time to time modified. No wonder, then, that those who confound the setting with the jewel—who fail to distinguish between forms of faith and the spiritual faculty itself, do not rightly honour this eye of the soul. On the other hand, the "religious" world ought not to call those "faithless" or "infidels" on whose souls the Spirit of God photographs pictures too wide for setting in traditional frames. Were it not that these two points are so frequently overlooked—first, that faith is not merely a theological virtue belonging as it does to all departments of thought and life; and secondly, that faith or the faculty by which spiritual things are discerned is very different from beliefs or those intellectual forms that stereotype the discoveries of faith, religious teachers would obtain a far more respectful hearing when they insist on the fact that it is the spirit and not the logical intellect which searcheth the deep things of God. Why should it seem in our verifying days a thing unreasonable that while God cannot be examined under a microscope, or detected by the surgeon's scalpel, He should nevertheless be verified every day and every hour by thousands of purehearted people who have cultivated their religious affections, and who are willing to *do* as soon as they *know* ? The mere logician seeks in vain for syllogisms amidst the delicate tinting and suggestive outlines of some masterpiece which is full of meaning, to the artist who considers both induction and deduction as so much verbiage. The man who has arithmetic rather than music in his soul may feel bored while listening to the purest melody, because he cannot count the notes as they are being played. We must have a "turn" for each art and study before we can appreciate them. What wonder, then, if such ideas as God, the Soul, and Immortality, should appear foolishness to those who attempt to see them by means of their intellect or human eyes, instead of by that faculty which is "likest God within the soul"? What wonder if this, the sublimest and most subtile part of man, should by continual disobedience to the laws of the kingdom of heaven, which are at least as imperative as those of the kingdom of nature, be so deranged that it would give to the careless inquirer no answer, or only a mocking one ?

" In every department of knowledge," says Robertson, "there is an appointed 'organ' or instrument for discovery of its specific truth, and for appropriating its specific blessings. In the world of sense, the empirical intellect—in that world the Baconian philosopher is supreme. His *Novum Organum* is experience: he knows by experiment of touch, sight, sound. The religious man may not contravene his assertions—he is lord in his own province. But in the spiritual world, the 'organ' of the scientific man —sensible experience—is powerless. If the chemist, geologist, physiologist come back from their spheres and say, we find in the laws of affinity, in the deposits of past ages, in the structure of the human frame, no trace or token of God, I simply reply, 'I never expected you would. Obedience and self-surrender is the sole organ by which we gain a knowledge of that which cannot be seen or felt.'"

How is it then with us, brethren? Have we this "vision and faculty divine?" Have we the prepared heart that enables us to see into the world which is unseen by the eyes of the body? All depends upon what we are, on what we bring with us—

> "Minds that have nothing to confer
> Find little to perceive."

No amount of evidence would substantiate the belief in a future state to a man who eats and drinks believing that to-morrow he dies, while to one who can say "I die daily," "faith is the substance— substantiates or makes real—things hoped for, the evidence of things not seen." And so truly reasonable and natural is this seeing of the soul or subjective experience, that it answers exactly to the process of bodily sight already referred to. We see our friends, our business, things that benefit us and things hurtful, and we act towards these on the assumption—for it is no more—that they are realities, not merely pictures on the retina of our eye; and so finding by experience that we avoid pain and receive pleasure from thus acting, we say that we know them to be real, having found them so by trust. Exactly so in a higher sense it is that faith substantiates things hoped for and trusted in.

Many are ashamed of believing in these sceptical days, and yet they *must* believe in much. Strictly speaking, there is no such thing as unbelief; and perhaps this is the reason why sceptical ages and men are generally superstitious. We may believe a thing not to be true, but this often implies far more credulity than in believing that it is true. This will be seen, if we consider how much we must believe in order to disbelieve in a God—we must believe "that this universal frame is without a mind." The alternative, therefore, is, whether we are more credulous in believing that things shaped themselves into their present, not surely, haphazard fashion, or that Chaos is guided into Cosmos by the piloting of God. Again, may it not tax our credulity more to believe that there is nothing in the evidences for Christianity, than that the religion is true? Before giving up beliefs from a desire of being considered intellectual, and from fear of being credulous, we should consider whether we are not more credulous in believing that what we reject is false, than in acknowledging it to be true, and may not, while straining at a gnat, swallow a camel. Scepticism and unbelief, as such, are anything but proofs of high mental powers, because deficiency in believing may show a want in the intellect as well as deficiency in doubting. In this way will come true the prediction concerning Him who is the brightness of His Father's glory, and the express image of His person—"He that believeth on Him shall not—even intellectually—be ashamed."

UNWIN BROTHERS,
THE GRESHAM PRESS,
CHILWORTH AND LONDON.

www.ingramcontent.com/pod-product-compliance
Lightning Source LLC
Chambersburg PA
CBHW032103220426
43664CB00008B/1122